ESSENTIAL MESSAGES FROM GOD'S SERVANTS

master*Work*®

Lessons from

THE OTHER SIDE OF LOVE

by Gary Chapman

THE GIFT OF FORGIVENESS

by Charles Stanley

SPRING *2006*

LifeWay.
CHURCH RESOURCES
Biblical Solutions for Life

Ross H. McLaren
Editor in Chief

Gena Rogers
Editor

Carolyn B. Gregory
Copy Editor

David Wilson
Graphic Designer

Melissa Finn
Lead Technical Specialist

John McClendon
Lead Adult Ministry Specialist

Mic Morrow
Adult Ministry Specialist

Send questions/comments to
  Editor, *MasterWork*
  One LifeWay Plaza
  Nashville, TN 37234-0175
  Or make comments on the web at
  www.lifeway.com

Management Personnel

Ron Brown and Larry Dry,
Managing Directors
Leadership and Adult Publishing
David Francis, *Director*
Sunday School
Bill Craig, *Director*
Leadership and Adult Ministry
Gary Hauk, *Director Publishing*
LifeWay Church Resources

Lessons by Gary Chapman are condensed from *The Other Side of Love* (Chicago: Moody Press, 1999). Used by permission of Moody Publishers.

Lessons by Charles Stanley are condensed from *The Gift of Forgiveness* (Nashville: Thomas Nelson Inc., 1991). Used by permission of Thomas Nelson Publishers.

Unless otherwise indicated, all Scripture quotations in the lessons from *The Other Side of Love* are from the Holy Bible, *New International Version*, copyright © 1973, 1978, 1984 by International Bible Society. This translation is available in a Holman Bible and can be ordered through Lifeway Christian Stores.

Unless otherwise indicated, all Scripture quotations in the lessons from *The Gift of Forgiveness* are from the *New American Standard Bible.* © The Lockman Foundation, 1960, 1962, 1963, 1968, 1971, 1972, 1973, 1975, 1977, 1995. Used by permission. This translation is available in a Holman Bible and can be ordered through Lifeway Christian Stores.

Quotations in the "How to Become a Christian" article or those marked HCSB are taken from the *Holman Christian Standard Bible®*, copyright © 1999, 2000, 2001, 2002 by Holman Bible Publishers. Used by permission. This translation is available in a Holman Bible and can be ordered through LifeWay Christian Stores.

Quotations marked NIrV are from the Holy Bible, *New International Reader's Version*, copyright © 1994, 1996 by International Bible Society. Used by permission of Zondervan Publishing House. All rights reserved. Quotations marked NKJV are from the New King James Version. Copyright © 1979, 1980, 1982, Thomas Nelson, Inc., Publishers. Scripture quotations marked (NLT) are taken from the Holy Bible, New Living Translation, copyright © 1996. Used by permission of Tyndale House Publishers, Inc., Wheaton, IL 60189 USA. All rights reserved.

MasterWork: Essential Messages from God's Servants (ISSN 1542-703X) is published quarterly by LifeWay Christian Resources of the Southern Baptist Convention, One LifeWay Plaza, Nashville, Tennessee 37234; James T. Draper, Jr., President, and Ted Warren, Executive Vice-President. © Copyright 2005 LifeWay Christian Resources of the Southern Baptist Convention. All rights reserved. Single subscription to individual address, $26.35 per year. If you need help with an order, WRITE LifeWay Church Resources Customer Service, One LifeWay Plaza, Nashville, Tennessee 37234-0113; For subscriptions, FAX (615) 251-5818 or EMAIL *subscribe@lifeway.com*. For bulk shipments mailed quarterly to one address, FAX (615) 251-5933 or EMAIL *CustomerService@lifeway.com*. Order ONLINE at *www.lifeway.com*. Mail address changes to: *MasterWork*, One LifeWay Plaza, Nashville, TN 37234-0113.

Printed in the United States of America.

Cover photo credit:
Comstock Images/PunchStock

table of Contents

Gary Chapman

masterWork:
Essential Messages from God's Servants

• Designed for developing and maturing believers who desire to go deeper into the spiritual truths of God's Word.

• Ideal for many types of Bible study groups.

• A continuing series from leading Christian authors and their key messages.

• Based on LifeWay's well-known, interactive model for daily Bible study.

• The interspersed interactive personal learning activities **in bold type** are written by the writer identified on the Study Theme unit page.

• Teaching plans follow each lesson to help facilitators guide learners through lessons.

• Published quarterly.

Gary Chapman, best known for his *Five Love Languages* series, is the author of numerous other books, including *Five Signs of a Loving Family* and *The Marriage You've Always Wanted.*

Dr. Chapman travels the world presenting seminars, and his nationally syndicated radio program airs on over 100 stations.

Dr. Chapman serves as senior associate pastor at Calvary Baptist Church in Winston-Salem, North Carolina. He and his wife Karolyn have two grown children.

AMY SUMMERS wrote the personal learning activities (**in bold type**) and teaching plans for this unit. Amy is an experienced writer for LifeWay Bible study curriculum, a wife, a mother, and a Sunday School leader from Arden, North Carolina. She is a graduate of Baylor University and Southwestern Baptist Theological Seminary (M.R.E.).

ABOUT THIS STUDY

Have you most often thought of anger as:
☐ **A curse?**
☐ **A personal weakness?**
☐ **A sin?**
☐ **A gift?**

Anger is God's gift to man and when handled biblically demonstrates both a reverence for God's holiness and a commitment to loving people.

Ask God to work through this study to help you learn to use His gift of anger to demonstrate reverence for Him and loving compassion to others.

The Other Side of Love

Processing Anger in a Godly Way

Learning to understand and process anger in a biblical way is part of being a follower of Christ. Anger is God's gift to man and when handled biblically demonstrates both a reverence for God's holiness and a commitment to loving people. When anger is processed properly, relationships are restored, wrongs are righted, and the world is a better place in which to live.

A biblical understanding of the origin and purpose of anger is the starting point for learning to manage anger. Remember, your capacity to experience anger is related to the fact that you are made in the image of God; as such, you have a concern for righteousness and fairness. With that in mind, you and I can face anger with a more positive attitude. Remember also that the true purpose of valid anger is to motivate you to take constructive action—to seek to right the wrong.

In reality, our anger is at the very heart of who we are. Tell me what you are angry about and I will tell you what is important to you. For the mature Christian, anger will focus on injustice, unfairness, inequity, and ungodliness; not on petty personal irritations. For the mature Christian such anger will motivate positive efforts to establish justice, fairness, equity, and godliness. His anger will be tempered with mercy and humility realizing that he too is capable of falling.

Such a lofty lifestyle—practicing justice, mercy, and humility in our daily lives—requires first that we reconcile with God through Christ; that gives us the motivation to aspire. Second, it requires the daily empowering work of the Holy Spirit, which enables us to succeed.

Of all peoples, the Christian has the greatest potential for understanding and processing anger to the glory of God. That is the message and goal of this study.

Gary Chapman

Understanding Anger

day One

What Is Anger?

First, let's seek to clarify what we mean by *anger. Merriam-Webster's New Collegiate Dictionary* (Sixth Edition) describes anger as "a strong passion or emotion of displeasure, and usually antagonism, excited by a sense of injury or insult." Although we normally think of anger as an emotion, it is in reality more than an emotion. Anger involves the emotions, the body, the mind, and the will, all of which are stimulated by some event in the individual's life.

We don't sit down and say, "I think I will now experience anger." Anger is a response to some event in life that causes us irritation, frustration, pain, or other displeasure. He comes home late; she fails to record a check; he fails to take out the garbage. You agree to meet at 6:30 p.m. It is now 7:30 p.m. and he or she has not arrived. Thousands of events have the potential for stimulating anger. Once the event has happened, the emotions respond.

> "Anger involves the emotions, the body, the mind, and the will."
> —Gary Chapman

Read the following passages. Draw a line from the passage to the event that stimulated God's anger.

Joshua 6:18-19; 7:1   Selfishness, rejecting truth, following evil

Judges 2:11-14   Disobedience of explicit commands

Romans 1:18   Evil and idolatry

Romans 2:8   Godlessness, wickedness, suppression of the truth

Typically anger is a cluster of emotions involving such feelings as disappointment, hurt, rejection, embarrassment, and other similar feelings. All of these clustered feelings we call anger. Anger is the emotion that typically pits you against the person, place, or thing that stimulated the emotion. It is the opposite of the feeling of love. Love draws you toward the person; anger sets you against the person.

The body also gets in on the experience of anger. The body's autonomic nervous system "gets the adrenaline flowing." Depending upon the level of anger, any or all of the following may happen physically. The adrenal glands release two hormones: epinephrine (adrenaline) and norepinephrine (nor-adrenaline). These two chemicals seem to give people the arousal, the tenseness, the excitement, the heat of anger. It is these physiological changes that give people the feeling of being overwhelmed by anger and being unable to control it.

Read the following passages. State the physical manifestation of anger displayed in each passage.

Exodus 11:8 _____

Job 15:12-13 _____

Acts 7:54 _____

The emotions, thoughts, and physiological changes are all intertwined. Together they compose what we call *anger*. Typically this anger is then expressed in behavior: words or actions. Although we have little control over our emotional and physiological responses to a troubling event, we can learn to control our thoughts—the way we interpret these events—and our behavior—our words and actions.

Later we will see how we can control and channel our thoughts and behavior. Our purpose at the moment is to clarify the components of anger. Anger is the emotions, thoughts, and physical tenseness we experience when we believe that something or someone is treating us or someone else unfairly.

"Anger is the emotions, thoughts, and physical tenseness we experience when we believe that something or someone is treating us or someone else unfairly."
—Gary Chapman

What Is the Origin of Anger?

Let's turn our attention to the question, What is the origin of anger? Or, to put it another way, Why do we experience anger? Anger is a pervasive human experience, and to know its source is the beginning of knowing how to deal with it.

I believe that the human capacity for anger is rooted in the nature of God. Please do not think that I am being disrespectful of God. On the contrary, I stand in deep reverence of God when I suggest that human anger is rooted in the divine nature. Further, I am not suggesting that anger is an essential part of the nature of God. I am suggesting that anger derives from two aspects of God's divine nature: God's holiness and God's love.

The Scriptures proclaim that God is holy (see 1 Pet. 1:16; Lev. 11:44-45.) The word *holy* means set apart from sin. Whether we are talking about God the Father, God the Son, or God the Spirit, there is no sin in the nature of God. The New Testament writer said of Jesus that He was "tempted in every way, just as we are—yet was without sin" (Heb. 4:15).

A second fundamental characteristic of the nature of God is love. John the apostle summarized the whole teaching of Scripture when he said simply, "God *is* love" (1 John 4:8, italics added). Please note that love is an adjective and not a noun. Love is not to be equated with God; rather, in His essential nature God is loving. This is not simply the New Testament concept of God. From beginning to end, the Scriptures reveal God as committed to the well-being of His creatures. It is God's nature to love.

It is from these two divine characteristics that God's anger is derived. Please note: The Scriptures never say, "God is anger." However, the Scriptures often indicate that God experiences anger. The word *anger* is found 455 times in the Old Testament; 375 of these times it is used of God's anger.

> "It is written, 'Be holy, because I am holy'" (1 Pet. 1:16, HCSB).

> "I am the LORD your God, so you must consecrate yourselves and be holy because I am holy. You must not defile yourselves by any swarming creature that crawls on the ground. For I am the LORD, who brought you up from the land of Egypt to be your God, so you must be holy because I am holy" (Lev. 11:44-45, HCSB).

Read Psalm 7:11 in your Bible. How often does God express anger?

_____

What aspect of God's character leads to His anger?

_____

Knowing the detrimental effects of man's sin, God's anger is stirred. It is God's concern for justice and righteousness (both of which grow out of His holiness and His love) that stimulate God's anger. Thus when God sees evil, God experiences anger. Anger is His logical response to injustice or unrighteousness.

Because God is holy and because God is love, God necessarily experiences anger. His love seeks only the good of His creatures. His holiness stands forever against sin. All of God's moral laws are based upon His holiness and His love; that is, they are always aligned with what is right, and they are always for the good of His creatures. God desires man to do what is right and enjoy the benefits. He said to ancient Israel, "I set before you today life and prosperity, death and destruction. For I command you today to love the Lord your God, to walk in his ways, and to keep his commands, decrees and laws; then you will live and increase, and the Lord your God will bless you in the land you are entering to possess" (Deut. 30:15-16).

So what does all of this have to do with human anger?

Read Genesis 1:27. What pattern did God use when He made humanity?

_____

We are made in the image of God. Though that image was marred by man's fall, it was not erased. People still bear the imprint of God's image deep within their souls. Thus, even though we are fallen, we still have some concern for justice and rightness. That is, people are moral creatures. In spite of modern man's attempt to reduce humans to an amoral creature, such a view is not consistent with reality. No matter how far a person may fall, he still has some concern for rightness.

What Is the Purpose of Anger?

Anger is the emotion that arises whenever we encounter what we perceive to be wrong. The emotional, physiological, and cognitive dimensions of anger leap to the front burner of our experience when we encounter injustice.

Why does a wife experience anger toward her husband? Because in her mind he has disappointed, embarrassed, humiliated, or rejected her. In short, "he has done her wrong." Why do teenagers experience anger toward parents? Because the teenager perceives that the parents have been unfair, unloving, unkind—that the parents have done wrong. Why do people get angry with electronic equipment? Because the equipment is not "working right." The machine, or its manufacturer, has done them wrong. Why do people blow horns when the traffic light turns green? Because they reason that the person in front of them "should be paying attention to the light and should have accelerated two seconds earlier." In short, they are not doing "right."

Think about a recent time you experienced anger. Why did you get angry?

_____

_____

_____

Chances are your answer will mention some injustice. Someone or something did not treat you fairly. Something was wrong. Your anger may have been directed toward a person, an object, a situation, yourself, or God, but in every instance someone or something treated you wrongly. We are not here discussing whether your perception of wrong is valid or invalid. We will deal with that later. What we are establishing here is that anger originates in the perception that something is wrong and that this sense of morality (some things are right and some things are wrong) finds its root in the fact that we are created in the image of a God who is holy and has established moral law for the good of His creatures.

Anger is not evil; anger is not sinful; anger is not a part of our fallen nature; anger is not Satan at work in our lives. Quite the contrary. Anger is evidence that we are made in God's image; it demonstrates that we still have some concern for justice and righteousness in spite of our fallen estate. The capacity for anger is strong evidence that we are more than mere animals. It reveals our concern for rightness, justice, and fairness. The experience of anger is evidence of our nobility, not our depravity.

We should thank God for our capacity to experience anger. When one ceases to experience anger, one has lost his sense of moral concern. Without moral concern, the world would be a dreadful place indeed.

Read James 1:20. Check the statement that best reflects the truth of this verse.
___ Anger is a sin and accomplishes nothing.
___ Anger that has its source in human selfishness doesn't accomplish what God desires.

Anger is a universal human experience, and God Himself often experiences anger. Those two facts lead us to conclude that there must be a foundational purpose for human anger. Since the capacity for human anger is a reflection of the image of the Creator, we are compelled to ask the question: What is God's purpose for human anger?

I believe the answer is clear: Human anger is designed of God to motivate us to take constructive action in the face of wrongdoing or when facing injustice. The reason this has not always been abundantly clear to Christians is that in our fallen estate, our perception of injustice is not always valid. That is, not all human anger is toward actual wrongdoing. The fact that our fallen nature is egocentric (centered on oneself) rather than theocentric (centered on God) often leads us to experience anger at anything that does not go our way. We will talk about valid and invalid anger in another session, but our purpose here is to return to the foundational question, "What is God's purpose in human anger?" The answer is: Anger is designed to motivate us to take positive, loving action when we encounter injustice. This, I believe, is illustrated by God Himself.

> "Human anger is designed of God to motivate us to take constructive action in the face of wrongdoing or when facing injustice."
> —Gary Chapman

Earlier today you were asked to think of a recent time you became angry. Did your response achieve God's purpose for human anger? ❏ **Yes** ❏ **No** **If yes, what did you do to express anger redemptively?**

_____

_____

If no, what could you have done differently to encounter injustice in a positive, loving manner?

_____

_____

day *Four*

What Is God's Response to Anger?

When we examine the record of God's anger in both the Old and New Testaments, we find that His patterned response always involves loving action. In the Old Testament, He typically sent a prophet to proclaim to the people His displeasure with their evil deeds and to call them to repentance. If the people repented, God's anger subsided and all was well. If, however, they did not repent, God took additional action. God's message to Jeremiah demonstrates this.

Read Jeremiah 3:12-14 and fill in the blanks.

God was _____ because Israel was _____.

God promised that if Israel would

_____

then He would _____.

Israel had forsaken truth and followed lies. God's anger motivated Him to send Jeremiah to call the people to repentance.

God took similar action in sending Jonah to Nineveh. The people of Nineveh knew God's reputation. When Jonah proclaimed the message of destruction in 40 days, the Scriptures say, "The Ninevites believed God. They declared a fast, and all of them, from the greatest to the least, put on sackcloth." Soon the king declared, "Let everyone call urgently on God. Let them give up their evil ways and their violence. Who knows? God may yet relent and with compassion turn from his fierce anger so that we will not perish." The people of Nineveh knew that God's anger was always driven by His love. So the Scriptures record, "When God saw what they did and how they turned from their evil ways, he had compassion and did not bring upon them the destruction he had threatened" (Jonah 3:5,8-10).

God's anger was expressed in positive action—declaring to the evildoers that all evil would be punished. Because of God's love for them, He could not allow injustice to go unpunished. However, when the people of Nineveh repented and turned from their evil ways, God's compassion forgave them. The wrong had been righted; God's anger had served its positive purpose. Throughout the Old Testament, this pattern of positive, loving action can be seen as God's response to anger. When people responded in repentance to the condemning message of God through the prophets, God always freely forgave. But when people did not respond and continued in their evil ways, God took further action—sometimes using swarms of locusts to eat the crops before harvest; sometimes famine and fire; sometimes foreign powers who would capture and take His people into slavery. But always the message was clear: God is doing this because of your sin. (See, for example, Amos 1–2.)

Some contemporary students of the Bible have questioned God's severe acts of judgment on His people Israel and their neighbors. They have read into these acts the picture of a severe God who has no love but only justice. However, upon closer examination, one discovers that when God used such severe measures it was for the ultimate good of His creatures. God's holiness will not allow Him to remain silent when men are involved in evil activity, and His love always seeks to express His anger for the larger good of mankind. When evil became so entrenched in a given culture and the people's hearts hardened to the call of God, God's judgment was severe in order to demonstrate to all the neighboring

"God's love always seeks to express His anger for the larger good of mankind."
—Gary Chapman

nations that such evil would not be tolerated forever. In destroying the cesspools of man's severe evil, God sought to prevent other nations from following the same destructive road. All His actions were just and all His actions were loving.

Read Psalm 30:5 as printed in the margin. How have you experienced God's anger for a moment?

"His anger lasts only a moment, but His favor, a lifetime. Weeping may spend the night, but there is joy in the morning" (Ps. 30:5, HCSB).

_____

_____

How have you experienced His favor for a lifetime?

_____

_____

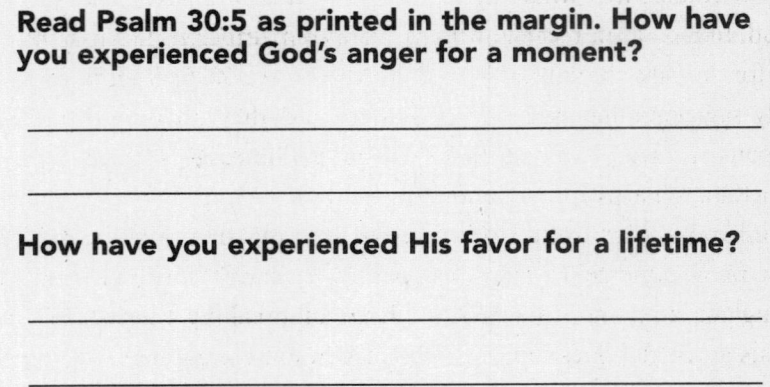

What Is Jesus' Response to Anger?

When we turn to the New Testament and examine the life of Jesus, we find that He too followed the same pattern in responding to His own anger. He took positive, loving action against the evil that had stimulated His anger. Perhaps the best known of these events was Jesus' experience in the temple in Jerusalem when He saw the merchants buying and selling oxen, sheep, and doves.

"It is written …
'My house will be called a house of prayer,'
but you are making it a 'den of robbers' "
(Matt. 21:13).

Read John 2:13-16 in your Bible and Matthew 21:13 in the margin. How did Jesus demonstrate His anger?

_____

What was the stimulus for Jesus' anger?

_____

Some would ask, "Where was Jesus' spirit of forgiveness?" We can without question assume that had they repented, He would have forgiven. But remember, God's forgiveness is always in response to man's repentance. His action demonstrated not only to the merchants but also to the religious leaders that what was going on was inappropriate for the temple of God. In fact, John records, "His disciples remembered that it is written: 'Zeal for your house will consume me' " (2:17; see Ps. 69:9). The disciples clearly saw Jesus' anger being expressed, and they attributed it to His righteous and deep concern that His Father's house be a place of prayer rather than a place of merchandise.

On another occasion Jesus was in the synagogue on the Sabbath, and a man came to Him with a paralyzed hand. The Pharisees were looking for an occasion to accuse Jesus of breaking the Sabbath law, so Jesus asked the question, "Which is lawful on the Sabbath: to do good or to do evil, to save life or to kill?" The Pharisees remained silent and Mark records that Jesus "looked around at them in anger and, deeply distressed at their stubborn hearts, said to the man, 'Stretch out your hand.' He stretched it out, and his hand was completely restored" (Mark 3:4-5). Jesus' anger was stimulated by the Pharisees' legalistic thinking, which placed the keeping of Sabbath laws above ministry to human need. His action was to heal the man in front of their faces, rejecting their evil thinking and graphically demonstrating in front of everyone that human ministry is more important than religious observances. Thus, the divine model is clear: God's response to anger is always to take loving action, to seek to stop the evil, and to redeem the evildoer.

OUR RESPONSE TO ANGER: TO SEEK RIGHTEOUSNESS AND REFORM

Now let's return to the human scene. I am not in any way suggesting that we are little gods. What I am suggesting is that we are creatures made in God's image and, because of that, we have at least on some level a concern for righteousness, fairness, and justice. Whenever we encounter that which we believe to be unrighteous, unkind, or unjust, we experience anger. I believe it is God's design that this anger motivate us to take positive, loving action to seek to set the wrong right; and where there has been a relationship, to restore the relationship with the wrongdoer. Anger is not designed to stimulate us to do destructive things to the people who

"God's response to anger is always to take loving action, to seek to stop the evil, and to redeem the evildoer."
—Gary Chapman

"Anger's fundamental
purpose is to motivate
us to positive, loving
action that will leave
things better than we
found them."
—Gary Chapman

may have wronged us nor does it give us license to say or do destructive things to our neighbors. Anger's fundamental purpose is to motivate us to positive, loving action that will leave things better than we found them.

Read Isaiah 58:6-7 in your Bible.

What should make God's people angry?

_____

What does God desire we do with that anger?

_____

Anger's purpose is to motivate us to respond to the injustices of life with constructive, loving action and do all that is in our power to see that justice prevails. Our actions, however, must always be guided by love.

During the Session

1. Invite participants to describe displays of anger they observed this past week. Ask: *What did those persons reveal was most important to them through their anger? What would your anger reveal about what's most important to you?* OR Instruct learners to think of a recent incident when they became really angry and try to recreate some of their physical reactions and thoughts from that instance. Instruct them to turn to a partner (maybe not their spouse if that's who they were mad at!) and, without divulging any personal confidences, share what they were experiencing physically and emotionally. *For either option:* Ask learners how they feel about themselves when they are angry. Ask participants if they agree or disagree with Dr. Chapman's declaration that anger is a gift and why they feel that way. Explain that this study of *The Other Side of Love* will help participants understand anger better and challenge them to use God's gift of anger the way God intends it to be used.

2. Request someone read Dr. Chapman's definition of anger in the margin on page 7. Ask: *Do you think anger just shows up out of the blue or is it always caused by some event? Explain.* Complete the first activity of Day 1. Ask learners which of the instances that stimulated anger within God have caused them to become angry. Ask learners how stimulants for their anger have changed as they have matured. Ask whether they think growing older helps a person handle anger in a more positive manner and why.

3. Dr. Chapman said the first step in dealing positively with anger is knowing the source of anger. Ask where anger is rooted. Direct learners to state two aspects of God's nature from 1 Peter 1:16 and 1 John 4:8 (printed on p. 8). Discuss the meaning of holiness and why that aspect of God's nature would result in divine anger.

4. Ask those who are parents if they've ever expressed anger at a child when the child did something that put him or her in danger. Explore how love was at the root of that parental anger. Comment that because parents love their children they are angry at anything that

To the Leader:

The teaching plan for each session will provide you two options for beginning the session. The first option will pose a question or two to help generate interest and discussion about the topic you will be studying that day.
The second option will be a little more physical or interactive.
The purpose of these suggestions, as with all the suggested teaching steps, is to spur your own thoughts to create interest and guide the discussion in a way that best fits the needs and personality of your class.

would harm them. Request learners follow along in their Bibles as you read Deuteronomy 30:15-18. Ask why God wanted His children to obey His commands. Request learners state what would happen if the people didn't obey God. Inquire: *Couldn't God display His love more fully if He blessed them regardless of their behavior? Explain.* [You don't display love to a child by rewarding him even though he ran into the street.] *How does God's anger actually display His love?* Explain that God is angry at sinful behavior because it harms His beloved children.

5. Ask someone to read Genesis 1:27. Explore what it means to be made in the image of God. Ask why being made in God's image leads to the human capacity to get angry. Invite someone to read the "anger is not ..." statements in the middle of Day 3 (p. 11). Ask whether any of those statements surprised learners and why. Ask why we should thank God for the capacity to experience anger.

6. Ask someone to read James 1:20. Explore how participants can reconcile that verse with the positive statements Dr. Chapman made about anger. Ask learners to state in their own words God's purpose for human anger. Explore why God's purpose is not often achieved in human anger. Encourage learners that this study will help them understand how to process anger in a way that does accomplish God's righteousness.

7. Request someone read Jeremiah 3:12-14. Ask why God was angry. Inquire: *Do you think God was angry for their sake or His? Explain. Do you think it's OK to get angry for your own sake? Why? How was God's anger expressed in positive action?*

8. Explain from Day 5 that God's response to anger is to take loving action, seek to stop the evil, and redeem the evildoer. Instruct learners to listen for how Jesus responded with those three steps as you read Mark 3:1-5. Call for responses. As time permits, lead learners to state specific situations when they would probably become angry and explore how they can apply God's response to anger to those situations.

9. Close in prayer that participants will learn how to please God with how they handle anger.

Productive Anger

day One

Make a Plan

Valid anger—anger that has been stimulated by genuine wrongdoing on the part of the other person—needs to be processed in a positive manner.

Read Proverbs 16:32 in the margin. Circle your answers below.

Does a mighty warrior take a city:

by rashly barging in OR with a careful plan?

Do you most often handle anger:

by rashly barging in OR with a careful plan?

> "Better a patient man than a warrior, a man who controls his temper than one who takes a city" (Prov. 16:32).

This week I would like to give a plan for processing anger in a constructive manner. Dealing with valid anger is a five-step process:

1. Consciously acknowledge to yourself that you are angry.
2. Restrain your immediate response.
3. Locate the focus of your anger.
4. Analyze your options.
5. Take constructive action.

Five Steps to Handling Valid Anger
1. Consciously acknowledge to yourself that you are angry.
2. Restrain your immediate response.
3. Locate the focus of your anger.
4. Analyze your options.
5. Take constructive action.

1. CONSCIOUSLY ACKNOWLEDGE YOUR ANGER

First, consciously acknowledge to yourself that you are angry. Because the emotion of anger comes on so suddenly, often we are caught up in a verbal or physical response to the anger before ever consciously acknowledging what is going on inside of us. We are far more likely to make a positive response to our anger if we first acknowledge to ourselves that we are angry.

I suggest that you say the words out loud. "I am angry about this! Now what am I going to do?" Such a statement places the issues squarely on the table. You are now not only aware of your own anger, but you have distinguished for yourself the difference between your anger and the action you are going to take. You have set the stage for applying reason to your anger rather than simply being controlled by your emotions. This is an important first step in processing anger positively.

As simple as this may sound, some Christians have difficulty with this. All their lifes they have been taught that anger is sin. Thus, to admit they are angry is to admit they are sinning. But this is not the biblical perspective on anger. I hope that the first session made it clear that the experience of anger is not sinful. It is a part of our humanity and reflects the anger experienced by God Himself.

> **Read Ephesians 4:26 in your Bible. What challenge did Paul issue to believers?**
> ❑ **Don't get angry.**
> ❑ **Don't sin when you are angry.**

That is precisely the topic we are addressing this week. "How do I keep from sinning when I am angry?" Or to put it in a positive way, "How do I respond to my anger so that my actions will be constructive?" Consciously and verbally acknowledging to yourself that you are angry is a first step in reaching this objective.

Gain Control

2. RESTRAIN YOUR IMMEDIATE RESPONSE.

If when we are angry we simply "go with the flow," we will likely have a negative and destructive response to anger. Very few adults have learned how to control and direct their anger. Most of us follow the patterns we learned in childhood by observing our parents or other significant adults.

These patterns tend to cluster around two extremes: verbal or physical venting or withdrawal and silence. Both are destructive. We will look at these and other patterns later.

For most of us, anger-control will be something we must learn as adults, and that means unlearning old patterns. Thus, restraining our immediate response is extremely important in establishing new patterns. Restraining our response is not the same as storing our anger. It is refusing to take the action that we typically take when feeling angry.

Read Proverbs 14:17; 19:11; and 29:11 and fill in the chart below.

Foolishness is associated with:	Wisdom is associated with:

Someone has said, "Speak when you are angry and you will make the best speech you will ever regret." Most of us have had the experience of saying or doing things in the immediate flush of anger that we later regretted but unfortunately were unable to erase. Far better to learn to restrain our immediate response.

Read James 1:19 in your Bible and fill in the blanks below, writing your name in the first blank.

_____ must be quick to _____,

slow to _____, and slow to _____.

From time to time I meet people in my seminars who say to me, "Dr. Chapman, I cannot control my anger. When I get angry, I am overwhelmed. I cannot restrain my response. I simply go berserk." While I am sympathetic with what the person is saying and I understand the overpowering nature of anger once it starts to roll, I believe that this is an ill-founded statement. It is true that once we begin to release anger in a destructive way verbally or physically, it's difficult to stop the flow of lava. But there is that moment before the red-hot words begin to flow that we can train ourselves to restrain that response.

"Don't sin by letting anger gain control over you. Think about it overnight and remain silent" (Ps. 4:4, NLT).

Did your mother give you this common sense advice? "When you are angry, count to 10 before you do or say anything." It is good advice, but many of us may need to count to 100 or even 1,000. This long delay may quell the fire within. Many have found this to be a workable technique in helping them restrain their response.

I suggest that you count out loud. If you are in the presence of the person at whom you are angry, I suggest you leave. Take a walk as you count. About halfway around the block when you come to 597, you will probably be in a mental and emotional state where you can stop and say, "I am angry about this. Now what am I going to do?" For the Christian, this is the time to pray, "Lord, You know that I am angry. I believe that what they have done is wrong. Please help me make a wise decision about how to respond in this situation." Then with God you begin to look at your options.

Another technique that I have often shared at my seminars is to call "time-out" when you realize you are angry. This may be expressed verbally by simply saying the words "time-out," or it may be expressed visually by the time-out sign often seen in athletic events on television in which outstretched fingers on both hands are brought together to form a T. It is your symbol for saying, "I'm feeling angry right now and I don't want to lose it, so 'time-out.'" If both of you understand that this is a positive technique and not a cop-out on the situation, you can accept this as a positive step in controlling anger. The time-out is not for three months; it is simply for a brief time to give you an opportunity to get in control of your emotions so you can approach the situation with constructive action.

State a specific time-out plan you will use the next time you get angry.

_____

_____

_____

_____

Get Perspective

3. LOCATE THE FOCUS OF YOUR ANGER.

Step three takes place as you are restraining your immediate response. While you are on your "time-out" and after you have counted to 100 or 1,000, locate the focus of your anger. If you are angry with your spouse, ask yourself the following questions: *Why am I so angry? Is it what my spouse has said or done? Is it the way he or she is talking? Is it the way he or she is looking at me? Does my spouse's behavior remind me of my mother or father? Is my anger toward my spouse influenced by something that happened at work today or in my childhood years ago?*

The secondary issue is, how serious is the offense? Some wrongs are minor and some are major. Each calls for a different response. To have the same response to minor issues as major issues is to mismanage one's anger.

You may find it helpful to rate the seriousness of the issue on a scale of 1 to 10, with 10 as the most serious of offenses and 1 a minor irritation. Numbering the level of offense will not only help you get it in perspective, but sharing the number with the persons at whom you are angry may prepare them mentally and emotionally to process the anger with you.

Think of the last time you became angry. On the scale below, rank how serious the offense seemed to you at the moment.

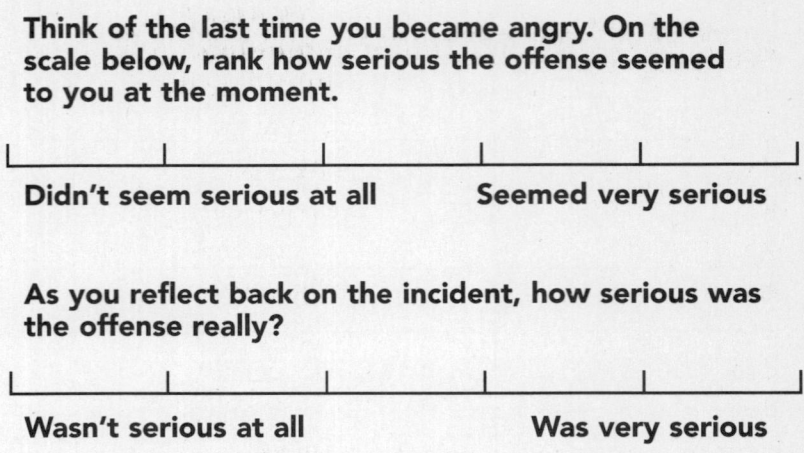

Didn't seem serious at all   **Seemed very serious**

As you reflect back on the incident, how serious was the offense really?

Wasn't serious at all   **Was very serious**

4. ANALYZE YOUR OPTIONS.

Locating the focus of your anger and the seriousness of the offense prepares you for taking step four: analyze your options. It is now time to ask the question: What are the possible actions I could take? As I see it, there are only two. One is to lovingly confront the person. The other is to consciously decide to overlook the matter. Let's look at the second option first.

There are times when the best Christian option is to admit that I have been wronged but to conclude that confronting the person who did the wrong holds little or no redemptive value. Therefore, I choose to accept the wrong and commit the person to God.

"Friends, do not avenge yourselves; instead, leave room for His wrath. For it is written: Vengeance belongs to Me; I will repay, says the Lord" (Rom. 12:19, HCSB).

"A man's wisdom gives him patience; it is to his glory to overlook an offense" (Prov. 19:11).

Read Romans 12:19 and Proverbs 19:11 in the margin.

What does God have the right to do when you are wronged? _____

What do you have the right to do when you are wronged? _____

When you release your anger to God, you are not stuffing or storing your anger. You are giving up the right to take revenge, which is always God's prerogative, and refusing to let what has happened eat away at your own sense of well-being. You are making a conscious choice to overlook the offense.

This is what the Bible calls *forbearance*, and it's turning the matter of justice over to God, knowing that He is totally aware of the situation. Thus, God can do to the individual whatever He judges to be wise. You are choosing not to be an emotional captive to the wrong that was perpetrated against you.

There are many other occasions in which overlooking the offense may be the best option. Our anger is released to God. The whole matter is placed in His hands, and we move on with our lives.

However, far more often the wise response to anger is to lovingly confront the person who has wronged you in an effort to seek resolution. We'll talk about that option tomorrow.

Forbearance—turning the matter of justice over to God.

day Four

Confront with Love

"If your brother sins, rebuke him, and if he repents, forgive him. If he sins against you … and says, 'I repent,' forgive him" (Luke 17:3-4). Notice that Jesus is talking about those with whom you have a relationship. He says, "If your brother sins … against you." Furthermore, the word translated to *rebuke* means literally "to set a weight upon." Thus, to rebuke is to lay a matter before someone, to clearly bring it to his or her attention.

Read Mark 8:31-33 in your Bible. What do you think Peter wanted to bring to Jesus' attention?

_____

What do you think Jesus wanted to bring to Peter's

attention? _____

_____

Peter rebuked Jesus because he thought Jesus misunderstood how a kingdom was to be established. Jesus rebuked Peter because He knew the disciple misunderstood reality. Peter was wrong and Jesus clearly confronted him with his wrong.

Rebuke is not verbal abuse. Rebuke is laying a matter before a brother whom you perceive to have wronged you. Such a rebuke needs to be done kindly and firmly, recognizing that there is always a possibility we have misunderstood the brother's words or actions as Peter misunderstood the words of Jesus regarding the Savior's approaching death. I often suggest that people write their rebuke before trying to speak it. It may go something like this: "I've got something that has been bothering me. In fact, I guess I would have to say I'm feeling angry. Perhaps I am misunderstanding the situation, but when you have an opportunity, I'd like to talk with you about it."

Such a statement reveals where you are, openly reveals your anger, and requests an opportunity to process it with the person involved. You have acknowledged up front that your perception may be imperfect, but at any rate, you want to get the issue resolved. Few people will not respond with an opportunity to talk about it if you approach them in such a manner. If given the opportunity, then you lay before them your perception of what you heard or saw or think to be true and ask if you are understanding the situation correctly. This gives the person an opportunity to share with you information that you may not be aware of or to explain his motives in what he did or said or to clearly admit to you that what he did was wrong and to ask your forgiveness.

Reconciliation with a friend or family member is always the ideal. Confronting is never for the purpose of condemning but rather for restoring the relationship to one that is genuine, open, and loving. If there has been a misunderstanding, the air is to be cleared so that we can go on fellowshiping. If wrongdoing is confessed, we are to forgive and the relationship is restored. The Apostle Paul wrote that we must always remember we may be the next one who offends (see Gal. 6:1). None of us is perfect and when we do wrong, we are likely to stimulate anger in the person whom we have wronged.

Loving confrontation is not easy for most people. We have had no training and very little experience in this approach to handling anger. We are far more experienced in either ventilating or seeking to deny or hide our anger, but such approaches are always destructive. Loving confrontation with a view to reconciliation is normally the best approach.

"Confronting is never for the purpose of condemning but rather for restoring the relationship to one that is genuine, open, and loving."
—Gary Chapman

Do you most often confront others to:
❑ **condemn?**   **OR**   ❑ **restore?**

Write a prayer asking God to give you the wisdom and power to confront with love.

_____

_____

_____

_____

_____

Move Forward

5. TAKE CONSTRUCTIVE ACTION

Once we have explored our options, it is time to take action. If you choose to "let the offense go," then you should share this decision with God. You might say something like this; "Lord, You know what has happened. You know how hurt I am, how angry I feel. But I really believe that the best thing for me to do in this situation is to accept the wrong and turn the person over to You. You know not only his actions but his motives. I know You are a righteous God, so I trust You to do what is right by the person. I also release my anger to You. The anger stimulated me to think through the situation, and I am taking the step I believe to be best. Therefore, the matter is over. My anger has served its purpose, and I release it to You. Help me not be controlled by any residual thoughts and feelings that come over the next few days. I want to use my life constructively and not be hindered by this event. Thank You that I am Your child and that You will take care of me."

If over the next few days or weeks your mind reverts to the wrong done to you and the emotions of hurt and anger return, take those thoughts and feelings to God and say, "Lord, You know what I am remembering right now, and You know the feelings I am feeling. But I thank You that I have dealt with that and I release these thoughts and feelings to You. Help me now to do something constructive with my life the rest of this day." Then you move out to face the challenges of the day.

On the other hand, if you choose the option of lovingly confronting the person who has wronged you, remember the challenge given by Paul.

Read Galatians 6:1 in your Bible. List the challenges you find in this verse.

_____

_____

Your confrontation may go something like this: "I have something that is bothering me, and I need your input. Is there a time we can talk?"

If your request is granted, you may say something like, "I'm feeling some hurt and anger over something that happened. I know I may be misunderstanding the situation. That's why I want to talk about it. Yesterday when you … I interpreted that as a very unkind action. I felt you weren't considering my feelings at all. Maybe I misunderstood your actions, but I need to resolve this." Perhaps the person will give an explanation that will shed light on his or her actions and give you a different perspective on the actions and the person's intentions. On the other hand, the person may admit that what he or she did was unthoughtful and unkind and may ask you to forgive him or her. In this case, you must always forgive.

If the offense was extremely grave in nature, forgiveness may not restore your trust in the person. We will discuss the nature of forgiveness later, but forgiveness is the promise that you will no longer hold this particular offense against the person. Your anger has served its purpose, and the two of you are reconciled.

Such loving confrontation typically results in either a genuine confession of wrongdoing and the extending of forgiveness, or the conversation sheds new light on the subject; you learn that what the person said or did was not exactly what you had perceived or that the motives were not the ones you had attributed to the person. In either case, the issue is cleared; the matter is resolved; and the relationship continues to grow. Anger has served its rightful purpose. It has motivated you to take constructive action to see that the issue was resolved.

If you presently have an unresolved conflict, what constructive action will you take this week?
❑ **I will choose to let the offense go.**
❑ **I will lovingly confront the person by**

_____

_____

To the Leader:

You may feel unqualified to teach these lessons because of your own struggle with anger. Good teachers aren't perfect Christians; they are humble, teachable learners. As you discover and obey biblical principles for handling anger, God will transform you. Then your class will learn from your life, not from your words!

Before the Session

Obtain a travel-sized tube of toothpaste and a paper plate (option: provide tubes of toothpaste for every participant).

During the Session

1. Encourage learners to name emotions. Write responses on the board. Lead a discussion on how each emotion can be productive or destructive. Ask if, in their experience, anger has been a mostly productive or destructive emotion. Explain that today you will look at a plan that, if followed, can transform angry feelings into productive action. OR Squeeze the entire contents of the tube of toothpaste onto a plate (or allow everyone to squeeze their own small tube). Then ask someone (or everyone) to put the toothpaste back into the tube. Ask how the toothpaste illustrates words or actions that sometimes come out of us when we are angry. Comment: *When we are squeezed, we often say or do things we regret. Today's study will challenge us to follow a plan that will lead us to express anger in a positive, productive way.*

2. Ask someone to read the five-step process from Day 1 (p. 19). Ask participants which step is the most difficult for them. Inquire: *Why is it not only important to state that you are angry but to ask yourself what you're going to do about that anger?* Explore why some Christians have difficulty acknowledging they are angry. Discuss the final activity in Day 1. Invite a volunteer to read Galatians 5:19-20. Inquire: *How can we reconcile Paul's statement that anger is not sin with his list of sinful behaviors which includes forms of anger?* Agree that uncontrolled anger, demonstrated in outbursts of rage, is what is denounced in these verses. The second step in Dr. Chapman's plan addresses this problem.

3. Ask someone to read Proverbs 29:11. Ask participants to describe what it means to give "full vent" to your anger. Inquire: *Why is the other man in this proverb wise—because he doesn't get angry? On a scale of 1 to 10, with 10 being very difficult, how difficult is it to restrain*

your immediate anger response? Ask participants to name habits that are difficult to break. Explore tricks people use to restrain themselves from indulging a bad habit. Emphasize that restraining an immediate response is necessary if you're going to establish new patterns of behavior. Ask someone to read Psalm 4:4 from the margin of Day 2 (p. 22). Ask how this verse instructs us to restrain our immediate anger response. Invite volunteers to share what "time-out" techniques work for them. Encourage learners: *Changing a habit is hard. Don't give up when you lapse into a destructive outburst of anger. Confess when you fail and ask God's help to succeed the next time.*

4. Lead participants to explore how locating the focus of their anger and analyzing the seriousness of the offense helps them gain perspective. Ask what two options we have when we have been offended. Discuss the second activity of Day 3 (p. 24). Guide participants to explore times when overlooking the offense may be the best option. Ask if they've ever overlooked the offense when they should have confronted the offender and why. (Option for classes with parents: Discuss whether overlooking a child's offense is ever an option and if so, when.)

5. Request someone read Luke 17:3-6. Ask: *Why do you need increased faith in order to rebuke someone?* Discuss what it means to rebuke someone and the purpose of loving confrontation. Read Luke 9:51-55. Ask why Jesus rebuked the apostles. Inquire: *Jesus could rebuke sternly and quickly. Why do we need to be more careful when we confront someone?* (Option for classes with parents: Discuss how parents can follow Dr. Chapman's encouragement in Day 4 to confront a young child with few verbal skills or a teenager who won't talk.)

6. Request learners read Galatians 6:1-5,9-10 in their Bibles and state all the challenges Paul gave believers. Write responses on the board. Discuss how obeying those challenges can help believers move forward when they've been wronged. Allow volunteers to share constructive actions they have taken that have empowered them to restore a relationship. Encourage participants who may be struggling with anger against someone to write their own version of the prayers in Day 5 on a small card and keep it with them to pray often throughout the day.

Distorted Anger

Understanding Distorted Anger

By this time you may be asking, "If anger is so positive, why has it caused so much trouble in the world?" The answer is as ancient as the garden of Eden. The drama revealed in Genesis 3 involving Adam and Eve, the serpent, and a fruit tree significantly changed man's nature. The face of God mirrored in the face of man is now distorted.

Anger is no different. The deceiver is still among us, and the scene of Eden is repeated daily. Perverting the divine purpose of anger has been one of Satan's most successful tactical designs.

The Enemy has used many strategies to mischannel God's intention for human anger. One of the most powerful is to make us think that all of our anger is of equal value; that is, that all of our anger is valid. "If I perceive that I have been wronged, then I have been wronged." This illusion leads us to conclude that whenever we experience anger, we "have a right to be angry."

Definitive anger is born of wrongdoing.

Two kinds of anger exist: definitive and distorted. *Definitive anger* is born of wrongdoing. Someone treats us unfairly, steals our property, lies about our character, or in some other way does us wrong. This is the only kind of anger God ever experiences. It is valid anger. The second kind of anger, *distorted anger*, is not valid. It is triggered by a mere disappointment, an unfulfilled desire, a frustrated effort, or any number of other things that have nothing to do with any moral transgression. The situation simply has made life inconvenient for us, touched one of our emotional hot spots, or happened at a time when we were extremely tired or stressed.

Distorted anger is triggered by things that have nothing to do with any moral transgression.

Read the following passages in your Bible. Circle the kind of anger you think the main character experienced in each instance.

Numbers 22:27-34   Definitive   Distorted

1 Samuel 20:30-33   Definitive   Distorted

Balak, king of Moab, hired Balaam to curse the Israelites. The Lord told Balaam not to do such a thing, but Balaam went with the officials from Moab. Balaam's donkey saw what Balaam did not see and refused to continue in the way, so Balaam beat the animal. When King Saul discovered his son Jonathan was cooperating with David, the king threw his spear at his son, trying to kill him. Both of these illustrations represent forms of distorted anger.

I call this *distorted anger*, not because the emotions are any less intense than those experienced with definitive anger, but because they are the responses to something less than genuine wrongdoing. Most of our anger with inanimate objects is distorted anger. The lawn mower did us no wrong. There is a mechanical explanation for why it will not start, but the lawn mower is not seeking to do us evil. The same is true with a flat tire, a wrench that keeps slipping off the bolt, a gas pilot light that refuses to ignite, etc. These experiences stimulate within us frustration and usually anger as well, but these inanimate objects did not choose to do us wrong.

Much of our anger with people is also distorted. What the person did frustrated us, disappointed us, hurt us, embarrassed us, but what he or she did was not actually wrong. Our anger experience may be just as intense as ever, but our response to such anger will be different from our response to definitive anger.

Give an example of a time you experienced:

Definitive anger _____

_____

Distorted anger _____

_____

day Two

Biblical Examples of Distorted Anger

Very early in Genesis we meet Cain, one of the sons of Adam and Eve. He worked in the fields as a farmer, while his brother, Abel, was a shepherd. In due time, they each brought an offering to the Lord—Abel a sheep and Cain some of the "fruits of the soil."

Read Genesis 4:4-5 in your Bible and fill in the blanks.

The Lord found favor with _____'s offering

but not with _____'s offering. So Cain

responded with _____.

A cursory reading may lead us to conclude that Cain had a right to be angry. Why would God reject his offering and accept that of Abel? Apparently, God had made it clear that they were each to bring an animal sacrifice. The importance of this is clear when we understand the rest of Scripture and the central role of the sacrificial lamb, Jesus, who is God's only plan of redemption. However, Cain decided to do it his way.

When we place human reason above God's clear commands, we have made a serious misjudgment. Cain followed his reason, offered his sacrifice, and experienced God's rejection. Then he blamed God with being unfair.

Read God's straightforward response to Cain in Genesis 4:6-7. Rewrite His response in your own words.

_____

_____

_____

Cain's anger toward God was not legitimate. It was not based on God's wrongdoing but rather on Cain's perception of wrongdoing. His experience of rejection and anger were real, but it was distorted. God's challenge was for Cain to deal with his own wrongdoing, release his anger, and come back into warm fellowship with God.

According to Genesis 4:8, how did Cain respond to God's overture? _____

Cain became the first of many who allowed distorted anger to control behavior and thus end up compounding their problems. The course of human history would have been much different if Cain had acknowledged that his anger was distorted, released it to God, repented of his own sin, and gone on with his farming.

Another example is Jonah. After Jonah's tumultuous sea voyage, he had made his way to Nineveh and proclaimed the clear message that God had given him: "Forty more days and Nineveh will be overturned" (Jonah 3:4). Much to Jonah's dismay, the people believed his message, declared a fast, and repented of their wrong deeds. Even the king took off his royal robes, covered himself with sackcloth, and sat down in the dust. He called upon the people to pray and turn from their evil ways in hopes that God would forgive and turn from His intentions. In keeping with His character, God had compassion and did not bring destruction upon the city.

When Jonah learned of this change of events, he was upset (4:1-3). Jonah was greatly embarrassed. He had proclaimed a message that now appeared to be untrue. *Why did God do this to me—interrupt my life in order to embarrass me? God knew that the people would repent. He has made me look like a fool. I'd rather die than live.* These must have been the thoughts that raced through the mind of Jonah.

Jonah's anger was illegitimate. It grew out of his own distorted thinking. He was focusing on himself and his reputation. He was relying on human reason rather than responding to truth. God had done him no wrong. In fact, had Jonah listened to God, he would have realized that he was privileged to be part of the good work God did in Nineveh. Rather than being embarrassed, he would have been honored.

Jonah allowed his distorted anger to control his disposition and lead him to the brink of suicide. The Scriptures do not tell where Jonah went

"Jonah was greatly displeased and became angry. He prayed to the Lord, 'O Lord, is this not what I said when I was still at home? That is why I was so quick to flee to Tarshish. I knew that you are a gracious and compassionate God, slow to anger and abounding in love, a God who relents from sending calamity. Now, O Lord, take away my life, for it is better for me to die than to live' " (Jonah 4:1-3).

from there. We can only hope that he listened to the word of the Lord, realized that his anger was based on faulty thinking, and returned home a faithful messenger of God.

The mind-set of distorted thinking says,

"It's all about _____."

More Biblical Examples of Distorted Anger

That people can recognize when anger is distorted and make positive responses is illustrated by the story of Naaman, a great military commander and valiant soldier who had leprosy. The commander had heard from a young girl, a prisoner of war, that a prophet in Israel could heal leprosy. Naaman immediately went to the king, told him what the young girl had said, and asked permission to go to the prophet in Israel. The king not only gave permission but encouraged Naaman in his pursuit. Naaman packed his gold, silver, and other gifts and headed off in search of healing.

Read 2 Kings 5:9-12 in your Bible. In your opinion, why did Naaman get so angry?

_____

Clearly, Naaman was an angry man. His blood pressure had risen. His nostrils were flared. His feet were stamping the dry ground. His anger quickly jumped to rage. In Naaman's mind, Elisha the prophet had done him wrong. He had a right to be angry. Instead, the prophet had actually given him a cure for his leprosy. Elisha had done him great good, but because Naaman's thinking was distorted, he was experiencing anger toward the prophet. In his rage, he was ready to return to his homeland, his mission not only a failure but a great embarrassment. Fortunately, there were some straight-thinking people traveling with him. See what Naaman's servants said to him in verses 13-15.

Naaman represents the person who experiences strong but distorted anger but who, when confronted, stops his rage and listens to reason rather than allow anger to control his behavior. As a result, this leader experienced healing and turned to honor the person at whom he had earlier been angry. The Story of Naaman demonstrates that distorted anger does not need to control our behavior and lead us to destructive acts.

Have you experienced distorted anger toward someone lately? ❏ **Yes** ❏ **No If yes, what has restored your reasoning about that situation?**

_____

_____

How will you return to and honor that person with whom you have been angry?

_____

_____

" 'Naaman's servants went to him and said, "My father, if the prophet had told you to do some great thing, would you not have done it? How much more, then, when he tells you, 'Wash and be cleansed'!" So he went down and dipped himself in the Jordan seven times, as the man of God had told him, and his flesh was restored and became clean like that of a young boy. Then Naaman and all his attendants went back to the man of God. He stood before him and said, 'Now I know that there is no God in all the world except in Israel. Please accept now a gift from your servant' " (2 Kings 5:13-15).

day *Four*

Processing Distorted Anger

If we are to have a wise response to anger, we must first discern whether that anger is based on actual wrongdoing. Questions must be asked and evidence must be weighed in order to process anger positively. These questions must be asked of yourself and sometimes of the other person.

The first question important in determining the validity of anger is, "What wrong was committed?" And the second is, "Am I sure I have all the facts?"

Two questions to determine the validity of anger:
1. What wrong was committed?
2. Am I sure I have all the facts?

All of us have had distorted anger based on a perceived injustice that never really happened. We can develop such anger in many ways: circumstantial evidence, faulty presuppositions, generalizations, our expectations or personal preferences, tiredness, and sometimes a combination of these factors. Whatever the cause, we conclude incorrectly that we have been wronged. We have an anger that is not valid.

So how do we address distorted anger, channeling it for the good? There are three essential elements in constructively processing distorted anger, often accompanied by a fourth. Today we will look at the first two elements.

SHARING INFORMATION

We begin by telling the other person our point of concern. This must always be done in a nonjudgmental manner. That's why I am calling it "sharing information." We are not sharing a verdict: "You let me down"; "You disappointed me"; "You didn't do what you promised." All of these are condemning, judgmental statements that tend to stimulate warfare. In contrast, "I'm feeling frustrated (disappointed, hurt, angry, or any other emotion), and I need your help" is a statement of information. It tells the other person what's going on inside of you, and it requests an opportunity to talk.

Sharing information rather than judgments is the first step in processing distorted anger. In sharing information, you focus on making the other person aware of your emotions, your thoughts, and your concerns. You focus on the event that stimulated your feelings, not on the person. You are more likely to be able to do this if you have first determined that the person has not wronged you. He may have made your life difficult, he may have caused you frustration, but he has not committed an immoral act.

"In sharing information, you focus on making the other person aware of your emotions, your thoughts, and your concerns."
—Gary Chapman

Think of the last time you became unreasonably angry with someone. Did you:
❑ **Jump in and judge that person's actions?**
❑ **Share information about your feelings?**

How might you handle a similar frustrating experience differently next time?

_____

_____

GATHERING INFORMATION

The second step is gathering information. Earlier we noted that on some occasions we will recognize we don't have all the facts. Therefore, it is difficult for us to determine whether our anger is definitive. Here's an example.

Meredith and Jason have a quick dinner, and she dashes out the door to attend her aerobics class. Three hours later, she returns home to find Jason on the couch watching television, the dirty dishes still sitting on the table where they left them. Meredith goes into an "anger attack."

Meredith has several options. If she understands the difference between definitive and distorted anger, she may begin by asking herself, "What wrong has he committed?" If she is wise, she will also ask the question, "Do I have all the facts?" An important step is to get information from Jason as to what has happened and why.

Going into the den, Meredith hugs Jason and says, "I have one small question before I give you a kiss. Why are the dirty plates still on the table?"

"Oh, Babe, I'm sorry," Jason answers. "I sat down here to watch the news. I meant to get the dishes right after the news but then the game started and the next thing I knew, I heard the garage door open. I must have been asleep for two hours. I'll get the dishes; I'm sorry. I must have been more tired than I realized."

Gathering information allowed Meredith to release her anger and perhaps even be glad that Jason was able to get some extra sleep. Gathering information is an important step in determining whether anger is definitive or distorted. When we realize that our perception of the situation is distorted, we can release that distorted anger and work on accepting others as human.

> "Gathering information is an important step in determining whether anger is definitive or distorted."
> —Gary Chapman

Read Matthew 7:1-2 from the margin. Besides the fact it is unscriptural, why is it a bad idea to judge someone for not being perfect, for making a mistake, or for doing something stupid?

> "Do not judge, so that you won't be judged. For with the judgment you use, you will be judged, and with the measure you use, it will be measured to you" (Matt. 7:1-2, HCSB).

_____

_____

Tomorrow we will discuss the third and fourth elements of processing distorted anger.

Continuing to Process Distorted Anger

NEGOTIATING UNDERSTANDING

The third step in processing distorted anger constructively is negotiating understanding. Sometimes even when our anger is distorted we cannot simply release it and accept what the other person has done. Often we need to negotiate understanding. Even when he or she has done nothing morally wrong, the behavior is still painful. You still feel disappointed, frustrated, hurt, and angry. You need to understand the other person's actions and you need for him or her to understand your feelings. This requires open conversation in a nonjudgmental atmosphere. Understanding that your anger is distorted should help you approach the conversation in a noncondemning way.

Rita and Doug both have vocations they find fulfilling. However, Rita has been experiencing a lot of anger toward Doug over the last six months. All of a sudden, he has become health-conscious. Three evenings a week after dinner he goes to the local gym to work out, leaving her with the dishes and the children. Her anger is growing into resentment. She doesn't like what she is feeling, and she certainly doesn't like what's happening to Doug. She feels that he is neglecting his responsibilities to help the children with their homework on those three nights. She feels that he is unthoughtful and unloving toward her and that he shows no concern for meeting her needs. Rita's anger is growing daily. She feels like she is about to explode. Doug seems to be happy, but she is extremely unhappy.

Rita's anger needs to be processed. She has held onto it far too long. Rita needs to share with Doug what is going on inside of her—her thoughts, her feelings, her frustrations—not in a condemning manner but as information. And she needs to find out from Doug how he perceives these things. This couple needs to come to a place of understanding, to find a way to meet all of their needs and to help them reconnect with each other emotionally.

Rita also needs to listen to Doug's response, not to try to counter what he says but rather to understand what he says. Then together they can seek to discover a way to meet her need for quality time with him, his need for physical fitness, the children's need for help with homework, and her need for a feeling of equity in household responsibilities.

Negotiating understanding is an important part of human relationships, whether the relationship is in the family, church, vocation, or any other area. All of us feel better about our relationships when we negotiate understanding. Even distorted anger indicates that something needs attention. Such anger seldom dissipates without open, loving communication between the parties involved.

Read Proverbs 2:1-6 in your Bible and complete the following:

Where is the first place we need to go to gain

understanding of a frustrating situation?_____

Record phrases from this passage that lead you to believe that understanding doesn't come easily or automatically.

_____

_____

What treasures do you gain when you work to negotiate understanding?

_____

_____

REQUESTING CHANGE

A fourth element in processing distorted anger exists that is often helpful: requesting change. In all human relationships, people will find certain behavioral characteristics irritating. Though the particular behaviors may differ, the resulting irritations often stir anger within us. For the most part, this anger is distorted in that the other person's behavior is not morally wrong; he or she has not perpetrated an evil against us. If the relationship is a close relationship and the person is one with whom we spend a great deal of time, it is sometimes helpful to seek to mitigate these irritations by requesting change. Please notice I say *requesting*, not demanding or manipulating. None of us responds well to those latter approaches.

In most relationships, assuming we feel loved and respected by the other person, most of us are willing to make changes if they are couched in the form of a request rather than a demand. Such requests and subsequent changes can alleviate many of the irritating behaviors that stimulate anger.

Distorted anger is no less real and is fully as disturbing as definitive anger. Both need to be thoroughly processed so that the anger does not build to resentment. The approaches are somewhat different. In my opinion, processing distorted anger is much easier than processing definitive anger. Finding constructive rather than destructive methods of processing both is our objective.

During the Session

1. Ask: *What rights do you possess as an American citizen? Do you always have those rights? Explain. Do you have the right to get angry? Do you always have the right to get angry? Why?* Explain that because of our sinful nature, some of our anger is distorted and not valid. OR Ask if participants have ever gone through a Hall of Mirrors. Ask: *What do the mirrors do? Would you want someone to evaluate your appearance based on those distorted images? Explain.* State that we must be careful not to express anger based on our distorted evaluation of a situation or a person.

2. Guide the class to explore the difference between distorted and definitive anger. Request participants share their responses to the first activity of Day 1 (p. 33). Inquire: *Do you think Balaam was angry only at the donkey? Why did he hit it? Do inanimate objects ever cause you to become frustrated? Why do we sometimes express anger at a person when we're frustrated with a machine? From the example of King Saul, how does distorted anger harm those we love and innocent bystanders?*

3. Ask someone to read Genesis 4:1-8. Lead a discussion with questions such as: *What did Abel do to Cain? Who was Cain really angry with? Was his anger valid? Why?* Request volunteers share their paraphrase of God's response to Cain in 4:6-7. Discuss how God's response refutes the declaration, "I just can't control my anger." Ask someone to read Jonah 4:1-9. Ask the class to state the reasons Jonah became angry and whether they were valid reasons. Explore what Cain and Jonah had in common. [Samples: They thought only of themselves; they were angry with God; they focused on human reason rather than truth; they let their distorted anger control them.]

4. Jump ahead to Day 4 for a minute and ask someone to state the two questions we can ask to help us determine the validity of our anger. Talk about what Cain and Jonah would have discovered if they had been willing to honestly ask those questions. Ask: *How can exploring those two questions when we feel angry actually change the course of our lives and the lives of others?* The biblical account of Naaman described

in Day 3 illustrates how lives can be changed for the better when persons are willing to listen to reason rather than their hurt feelings. Discuss the first activity of Day 3 (p. 36). Invite someone to read 2 Kings 5:13-15 from the margin on page 37. Ask: *What do you admire about Naaman? How can we: (1) gently help someone else see reason in their anger and (2) humbly listen to someone who's trying to reason with us?* Invite volunteers to share their responses to the last activity in Day 3.

5. Ask the class to state from Day 4 the first two elements in constructively processing distorted anger. Ask: *When we are enraged with distorted anger, what is our focus in communication? What is the focus in sharing and gathering information?* Review the illustration about Meredith and Jason. Ask what Meredith might have said to Jason if she had not chosen to process her anger positively and how Jason might have responded. Ask: *Was Jason morally wrong because he neglected to clean up? Explain. Did Meredith have the right to get angry? Why? Would Meredith have been morally wrong if she had not accepted his explanation? Why?* Discuss the final activity of Day 4 (p. 39). Ask: *What happens when you judge a situation before gathering all the information? In your experience, if you give others a break for being human, do they give you a break as well?*

6. Remind participants of the illustration of Rita and Doug from Day 5. Ask: *Do you think Rita has a valid reason to be angry? Why?* Discuss how Rita can share and gather information with Doug. Then ask what the couple must do after they grasp the situation. Discuss the activity on page 41.

7. Acknowledge that not everyone is going to resolve their issues as easily as the illustrations in today's study. Sometimes one party will not be willing to share information or negotiate an understanding. Remind participants they are responsible only to try to resolve the issue and then they must give their anger to God. Encourage them that the distorted "face of God mirrored in the face of man" will one day be restored. Read 1 Corinthians 13:12. Close in prayer.

Responding to Anger

day One

Explosive and Implosive Anger

The flame shot upward, fueled by a break in a city gas line. The line had ruptured when a private contractor, clearing land, clipped a gas pipe. At first just the pressurized gas poured out, hissing loudly. But within 30 minutes, a random spark had ignited the natural gas, which flamed skyward.

Within minutes the fiery plume was almost five stories high and only a few yards away from Chicago public housing that lodged senior citizens. Fortunately, police and others evacuated the residents from the building. But when the gas company finally stopped the fuel feeding the line, scores of people had been displaced, their housing gutted or scorched.

Two months later, in December 1998, another explosion would displace Chicago residents. This time, though, the explosion was planned. A series of dynamite charges rigged by a demolition company popped in succession, and, one by one, four adjoining buildings at a different public housing project fell, crumbling to the ground and raising huge clouds of dust.

The difference was this explosion was actually an implosion, with building materials falling inward; and the destruction had been planned for months, as the run-down housing would be replaced with various scattered housing. In fact, former residents and other spectators watched a safe distance away, some oohing and aahing, and many even applauding.

Which do you think was the more destructive event— the explosion or the implosion? Underline your response and explain your answer below.

_____

_____

Many would say the most destructive was the gasoline explosion that charred the side of a building and left people without homes. This devastation was unplanned and people had no alternative housing. In the case of the demolished public housing, most of the displaced residents already had arranged for replacement housing.

In truth, both the gas explosion and the building implosion had equally destructive consequences. In fact, with the implosion, more buildings fell, greater dust and debris gathered, and many of the former residents regretted leaving the apartment housing that for years they had called home. Their emotional loss and personal pain were no less.

Similarly, there are two equally devastating responses to anger: explosion and implosion. We may think that one is more destructive than the other, but the truth is implosive anger can be as damaging as explosive expressions of anger. Both can occur at varying levels of intensity, yet either response has destructive consequences. They represent destructive ways of responding to anger.

We have looked at constructive ways of responding to anger the last three weeks. But let's be honest, many of us have never learned to handle anger positively. Our responses to anger in the past have always made things worse. We find it hard even to believe that anger itself is not evil.

Our increasingly violent culture is no doubt the result of multiple causes, but one of those would certainly be uncontrolled anger. That is our focus this week: recognizing the negative responses and rejecting them in favor of constructive ones.

"A man who does not control his temper is like a city whose wall is broken down" (Prov. 25:28, HCSB).

Read Proverbs 25:28 from the margin. Choose the statement below that you think best reflects the truth of this verse and give a reason for your choice.

Uncontrolled anger:

is destructive because: _____

leaves you vulnerable because: _____

leaves a big mess because: _____

day Two

Recognizing Explosive and Implosive Anger

EXPLOSIVE ANGER

First, we will examine explosive anger. For many, this is their predictable response to anger. Explosive anger expresses itself in two modes: words and actions. Verbal abuse and physical abuse are household words in America. What is even more painful is that most of us have either given or received one or both of these. Uncontrolled anger is at the root of all such abuse.

Explosive anger expresses itself in two modes: words and actions.

Explosive, angry behavior is never constructive. It not only hurts the person at whom it is directed, it destroys the self-esteem of the person who is out of control. No one can feel good about himself or herself when he or she thinks about what he or she has done. In the heat of such angry explosions, people say and do things they later regret. Undisciplined anger that expresses itself in verbal and physical explosions will ultimately destroy relationships. The person who receives such angry explosions loses respect for the person who is out of control and will eventually lose any desire to be in his or her presence.

Read Genesis 49:5-7 in your Bible. If you were to ask Jacob why he didn't enjoy being with his sons Simeon and Levi, how would he have responded?

_____

_____

Some years ago it was popular in certain psychological circles to believe that releasing anger by aggressive behavior could be a positive way of processing anger if the aggression was not toward a person. Thus, angry people were encouraged to beat pillows, punching bags, and dolls or to take their aggression out on a golf ball. However, almost all research now indicates that the venting of angry feelings with such aggressive behaviors does not drain a person's anger but actually makes the person more likely to be explosive in the future.[1] Explosion, whether verbal or physical, is not an acceptable way of handling one's anger.

IMPLOSIVE ANGER

Merriam-Webster's New Collegiate Dictionary (Sixth Edition) defines *implosion* as "a bursting inwards; contrasted with explosion." In destroying any building through implosion, the wrecking crew places the destructive power within the building rather than outside, keeping all the rubble and glass inside. This is a graphic picture of what happens to the person who chooses to hold anger inside. One's life literally crumbles around internalized anger. Whereas explosive anger is readily observed by the person's screaming, swearing, condemning, criticizing, and other words or acts of rage. Implosive anger is not readily recognized by others because it is, by definition, held inside.

Implosive anger is not readily recognized by others because it is, by definition, held inside.

Read Leviticus 19:17 from the margin. Does this verse warn against ❏ explosive or ❏ implosive anger? (Check your answer.)

"You must not hate your brother in your heart. Rebuke your neighbor directly, and you will not incur guilt because of him" (Lev. 19:1, HCSB).

In the verse printed in the margin, circle the antidote to implosive anger.

What will eventually happen to you if you hold in your anger rather than process it positively?

_____

Some Christians who would deplore explosive expressions of anger fail to reckon with the reality that implosive anger is fully as destructive in the long run. Whereas explosive anger begins with rage and may quickly turn to violence, implosive anger begins with silence and withdrawal but in time leads to resentment, bitterness, and eventually hatred. Implosive anger is typically characterized by three elements: denial, withdrawal, and brooding. We will look at each of these elements tomorrow.

Characteristics of Implosive Anger

As you read the three elements of implosive anger, underline any statements that describe how you have handled your anger at times.

DENIAL

Those who practice an implosive method of responding to anger often begin by denying they are angry at all. This response to anger is especially tempting to Christians who have been taught that anger itself is sinful.

Denying anger does not eliminate its destructive power. Internalized anger, whether admitted or not, will have its destructive effect on the body and the psyche of the angry individual. The anger does not die with denial. Rather, it continues to expand until denial is no longer possible.

WITHDRAWAL

While denial is often but not always a characteristic of implosive anger, withdrawal is the central strategy of the person who practices implosive anger. While admitting anger to themselves and to others, they withdraw from the person or situation that stimulated the anger. The idea is not denial but distance. *If I can stay away from the person or at least not talk to him when I am with him, perhaps my anger will diminish with time*, the angry individual reassures himself. If the offending person notices the silent withdrawal and asks, "Is something wrong?" the withdrawer will respond, "No. What makes you think something's wrong?" If the person pursues by asking, "You've been quieter than usual," the withdrawer may respond, "I'm just tired. I had a hard day," as he walks out of the room.

BROODING

A third characteristic of implosive anger is brooding over the events that stimulated the anger. In the person's mind, the initial scene of wrong-doing is played over and over like a videotape. He sees the other person's facial expression; he hears the person's words; he senses his spirit;

he relives the events that stimulated the angry emotions. He replays the psychological audiotapes of his own analysis of the situation.

How could he be so ungrateful? Look at the number of years I've put into the company. He's only been here five years. He has no idea what's going on. If he knew how important I am to the company, he wouldn't treat me this way. I feel like resigning and letting him suffer. Or I feel like appealing to the board and getting him fired.

On and on the tapes play as one wallows in his or her anger. The difficulty is the tapes play only in the angry person's head. The anger is never processed with the person involved or with a counselor or trusted friend. The anger is developing into resentment and bitterness. If the process is not interrupted, the person will eventually experience an implosion in the form of an emotional breakdown, depression, or in some cases, suicide.

However, for a growing number of these people who are internalizing anger, the end result will be not an implosion but an explosion. In their desperate emotional state, they will commit some act of violence toward the person who wronged them. Implosive anger is fully as destructive as explosive anger. That is why the Scriptures always condemn internalizing anger.

> "Now is the time to get rid of anger, rage, malicious behavior, slander, and dirty language" (Col. 3:8, NLT).

> "Get rid of all bitterness, rage, anger, harsh words, and slander, as well as all types of malicious behavior" (Eph. 4:31, NLT).

Read Colossians 3:8 and Ephesians 4:31 from the margin. Underline what the Apostle Paul directed believers to do with their anger.

Read Ephesians 4:26-27 in your Bible. What is the danger of letting anger live inside you for a while?

_____

_____

> "Anger was designed to be a visitor, never a resident in the human heart."—Gary Chapman

Solomon warned that "anger resides in the lap of fools" (Eccl. 7:9). The key word is *resides*; the fool lets the anger abide in him. The implication is that those who are wise will see that anger is quickly removed. Anger was designed to be a visitor, never a resident in the human heart.

Results of Implosive Anger

The silent, withdrawing approach to anger may last for a day or for years, but the longer this approach is taken, the more certain is resentment and bitterness.

Often this internalized anger will express itself in what the psychologists call passive-aggressive behavior. The person is passive on the outside, trying to give the appearance that nothing is bothering him, but eventually the anger is expressed in other ways, such as failure to comply with the request the other person makes.

Another common result of internal anger is to redirect the buried anger. The individual redirects his or her angry feelings away from the person or situation that stimulated the anger and toward another person or object. Such expressions of misplaced anger do not process the original anger. It is still buried inside the person, waiting to be processed in a more positive manner.

This suppression of anger, holding anger inside, will eventually lead to physiological and psychological stress. There is a growing body of research that shows a positive correlation between suppressed anger and physical ailments. However, the more pronounced results of suppressing anger are found in its impact on one's psychological or emotional health.

Eventually the emotions of hurt from the internalized anger are replaced. In their stead appear the emotion of bitterness and the attitude of hatred. Almost always those who hate wish ill on the person at whom they are angry. Sometimes they end up perpetrating this ill themselves. The internalized anger erupts for all the world to observe.

When someone perpetrates evil upon the individual who wronged him, he has taken the prerogative of God. When we seek to impose judgment on those who have wronged us, we will inevitably make things worse.

"Do not say, 'I'll pay you back for this wrong!' Wait for the LORD, and he will deliver you" (Prov. 20:22).

Read Proverbs 20:22 from the margin. When someone wrongs you, which of the following do you do most often? Check one.
❏ **Act immediately to make the person pay**
❏ **Stew a while and then make the person pay**
❏ **Wait for God to right the wrong**

DEFUSING IMPLOSIVE ANGER

What positive steps can one take to defuse implosive anger? First, admit the tendency to yourself. Second, reveal your problem to a trusted friend or family member. Telling someone else and asking for their advice may help you decide whether you should confront the person or persons with whom you are angry. Perhaps you will choose to let the offense go, but at least this will be a conscious choice, and you can release your anger. If the person to whom you disclose your anger is unable to give you the help you need, then look for a pastor or counselor who can. Don't continue the destructive response to anger.

The clear challenge of Scripture is that we learn to process anger in a positive, loving manner rather than by explosion or implosion.

"The clear challenge of Scripture is that we learn to process anger in a positive, loving manner rather than by explosion or implosion."
—Gary Chapman

Read Psalm 37:1-9 in your Bible. We are repeatedly admonished not to _____ because it only leads to _____. Instead we are to

_____

The practice of explosive anger and implosive anger are not only highly destructive to the individual who is so handling anger but to everyone involved, including the community at large. Neither of these responses to anger can be accepted as appropriate in the life of a Christian. If you recognize either of these patterns in your own response to anger, I urge you to talk with a pastor, a counselor, or a friend; share with someone your struggle with these destructive patterns. You cannot reach your potential for God and good in the world if you continue to respond to your anger either by explosion or implosion.

This brings us to the next issue in handling our anger: What about the person who has been wronged for a lifetime and has stored the anger inside and has become an angry, resentful person?

Dealing with Stored Anger

Whenever we are wronged, anger is the natural emotion that arises within. The healthy way of handling that anger is to lovingly confront the person who has wronged us and work through it, seeking a resolution. Often, however, because of various circumstances, we are not able to do that. Children, for example, seldom process their anger toward parents—usually out of fear that the parents will not understand or will make things even worse.

Wrongs are not forgotten unless they are processed. The fact that we can remember these several years after they happened indicates we have not really forgotten them.

Whenever we have experienced a series of wrongs over a long period of time, our emotional ability to absorb these wrongs is stretched beyond capacity. One of two things begins to happen. We begin to express this anger not toward the people who perpetrated it through the years but toward other people in our present setting.

The purpose of our anger is to motivate us to take constructive action with the person who has wronged us, but if we fail to do this, unresolved anger becomes a dark cloud over our lives. We have been wronged throughout our lives by numerous people in numerous ways. The heaviness of all that injustice begins to settle on our emotions. And we find ourselves becoming lethargic toward life, no longer interested in the things that used to stimulate our interest. If positive steps are not taken, we can go on to become more and more explosive and/or more and more depressed.

God is loving and God is just. God cares about the well-being of His creatures, but God ultimately will bring all persons to justice. The cross is all about Christ who took the full penalty of our sins. And those who will accept that, God can forgive and still be just (see Rom. 3:26).

The Scriptures say, "Vengeance is mine; I will repay, saith the Lord" (Rom. 12:19, KJV). It is never our job to vindicate ourselves by making people pay for the wrongs they've done toward us. They will either confess those wrongs to God and experience His forgiveness based on what Christ has done for them, or they will face God with those sins and He will be the ultimate and final judge.

"See to it that no one repays evil for evil to anyone, but always pursue what is good for one another and for all. Rejoice always! Pray constantly. Give thanks in everything, for this is God's will for you in Christ Jesus" (1 Thess. 5:15-18, HCSB).

Read 1 Thessalonians 5:15-18 from the margin.

Think of someone with whom you have been angry and consider the following:

1. How will you pursue what is good for that person?

_____

_____

2. Why can you rejoice even though you are hurt?

_____

_____

3. How will you pray for this person and situation?

_____

_____

4. Why can you give thanks for this painful circumstance?

_____

_____

WHEN ANGER CONTINUES FOR THE LONG TERM

After 25 years of counseling, I am convinced there are thousands of people in the world who go for many years untroubled by their hidden anger. But sooner or later, unprocessed anger will express itself either in violent behavior normally toward innocent people or in deep, unresolved depression that keeps the individual from reaching his or her potential for God and good in the world. Please do not hear me saying that all depression is caused by unresolved anger. This is certainly not the case. But depression is sometimes the result of anger that is stored inside the individual over a long period of time.

When anger remains for the long term, we must process it to avoid those explosive or implosive responses. Making a list of the wrongs perpetrated against us through the years is the first step in identifying unprocessed anger. Once the list is made, we may ask ourselves, "How did I process my anger over this event?" If we find that it was not processed or that it was processed poorly, then it is never too late to deal with unresolved anger.

> "It is never too late to deal with unresolved anger."
> —Gary Chapman

On a separate piece of paper prayerfully answer these questions:

1. Who are the people who have wronged me?
2. What have they done?

Then read out loud to God every name and offense, releasing each of them to Him.

You may choose to burn the paper as a physical indication of the release of your anger. Or keep the list and as you see God working in each relationship make a note of it next to the person's name.

Processing our anger with God in this manner does not in and of itself rebuild relationships with the people who have wronged us. Rather it brings emotional and spiritual healing to us. Equally important, it makes our lives different in the future.

Whether we should go back and seek to deal personally with the individuals who wronged us is a decision that requires prayer and careful thought. Where this can be done, it brings the potential not only of personal healing but of healing the relationship. At the same time, it brings the potential for further rejection, hurt, and wrong. If the person is still alive and the relationship is still important, I recommend one prayerfully consider this alternative. Usually such an attempt at reconciliation will be more productive if the individual has the assistance of a trusted pastor, counselor, or friend. Such reconciliation always requires forgiveness.

---

[1] Mark P. Cosgrove, *Counseling for Anger* (Dallas: Word, 1988), 71, 95.

Meditate this week on Psalm 37. How will you trust, delight in, and commit yourself to the Lord? Take time to be still and wait on Him. How do those actions and attitude of trust help you refrain from anger and fretting? Be prepared to share your personal experiences with your class.

Before the Session

1. Obtain a paper bag and three balloons. Recruit three volunteers to blow up the balloons.
2. Be prepared to summarize Genesis 34.

During the Session

1. Ask participants if they have ever observed an implosion and if so, describe. Ask: *What's the difference between an explosion and an implosion? How are they the same? Why did Dr. Chapman use explosion and implosion to describe two negative ways people respond to anger? Which do you think is the most destructive? Why?* Remark that if we should not blow up with anger or stuff it inside, then we must find a positive way of getting rid of our anger. OR Instruct the volunteers to blow up their balloons and hold them closed with their fingers. Tell the class the air inside the balloons represents anger. Pop one balloon with a pin. Ask if the best way to deal with anger is to pop and let it all out. Tie another balloon closed and put it into the paper bag. Ask if the best way to deal with anger is to stuff it inside where you can't see it. Request participants give reasons for their responses. Finally, ask the third volunteer to open his or her fingers slightly to release air from the last balloon. (Tell the person not to let go of it, you don't want it flying all over the room!) Remark that today's study will challenge us not to explode or implode with anger but to release our anger to God.
2. Ask someone to read Proverbs 25:28 (p. 46). Comment that whether the city wall exploded or was imploded, it was still destroyed. Discuss the final activity of Day 1. Assure learners there is no one right answer.
3. Instruct participants to describe typical characteristics of explosive anger. Ask how explosive anger harms the angry person and the person at whom the anger is directed. Discuss the first activity of Day 2. Explain that Jacob was referring to a time Simeon and Levi exploded with anger. Summarize Genesis 34:1-24. Invite someone to

read Genesis 34:25-31. Ask: *Did the brothers have the right to get angry? Did they have the right to respond the way they did? Who was harmed by their explosive anger?* Lead the class to discuss ways to restrain explosive anger. Refer them back to the five-step plan discussed in Week 2 (beginning on p. 19).

4. Ask learners to define implosive anger. Review the three characteristics of implosive anger from Day 3 (p. 49). Discuss why denial or withdrawing from anger is destructive. Read Ecclesiastes 7:9. Discuss learners' interpretation of Dr. Chapman's statement, "Anger was designed to be a visitor, never a resident in the human heart." Discuss the final activity of Day 3. Explore how unresolved anger gives Satan an opening in a life.

5. Discuss who is hurt by implosive anger and how. Ask why we make things worse when we seek to impose judgment on those who have hurt us. Ask for volunteers to read Proverbs 20:22 and Psalm 37:1-9. Lead a discussion about what we are to do and not do when we are wronged. Explore what it means to wait on the Lord and how that is possible when we are so angry and hurt.

6. Dr. Chapman is convinced that numerous persons go untroubled by hidden anger for years only to have it erupt with explosive or implosive results. Ask learners if they have observed that to be true. Ask how one can recognize the signs of long-term anger. Explore what might trigger a destructive response to anger that has been buried for ages. Inquire: *What's the only way we can assure that we won't explode over some anger that occurred so long ago we almost have forgotten about it? What are ways Dr. Chapman said we can release anger positively?* [See "Defusing Implosive Anger" in Day 4 and all of Day 5 to help answer this question.]

7. Relate this case study: *Mary grew up in a good home, but as she's gotten older she finds herself feeling more and more angry at the memory of times her family, perhaps unknowingly, hurt her feelings or ignored her needs.* Ask how this stored up anger might be exhibiting itself in Mary. Ask someone to read 1 Thessalonians 5:15-18. Explore how obeying these biblical commands can help Mary resolve this anger before it does further damage to her and to others.

Anger and Forgiveness

day One

Separation ... and Forgiveness

When one person sins against another, it creates distance between them. This reality is evidenced throughout Scripture, beginning with Adam and Eve, who before their sin enjoyed fellowship with God in the garden. But after their sin, they found themselves not only hiding from God but estranged from each other. Adam was blaming Eve; Eve was blaming the serpent. That's not exactly a picture of domestic tranquility.

Read Isaiah 59:2 and Romans 6:23 in your Bible. List the consequences of sin.

_____

_____

> "God desires fellowship with His creatures. That is what the cross of Christ is all about."
> —Gary Chapman

We are never separated from God's love, but sin does separate us from His fellowship. Death is the ultimate picture of separation. This is not what God desires for His creatures; therefore, the writer of Romans quickly adds, "The gift of God is eternal life in Christ Jesus our Lord" (Rom. 6:23). God desires fellowship with His creatures. That is what the cross of Christ is all about. God offers His forgiveness and the gift of eternal life.

In order to experience God's forgiveness, man must respond to the call of God's spirit by repentance and faith in Christ (see Acts 2:37-39). The word *repent* means literally "to turn around." The message is clear: If we are to receive God's forgiveness and enter into His eternal family, we must turn from our sin, acknowledge that Christ has paid the ultimate penalty for our sins, and accept God's forgiveness and gift of eternal life— all of this at the urging and guiding of the Holy Spirit.

The Scripture describes this new believer in Christ as "a newborn baby" who must grow up into Christlikeness. God's objective is clear: He wants His children to become like Christ (see 1 Pet. 2:2-5,9-12; Rom. 8:29). However, this does not happen instantly. It is a process, and because our sinful nature is not eradicated, there is always the possibility that we will momentarily turn from God's purposes and fail to follow the teachings of Jesus. Again the biblical word for this failure is *sin*.

Read 1 John 1:9 in your Bible. Complete the if/then statement below to identify your responsibility and God's promise when you fail Him.

If _____,

then _____.

In order for our fellowship with God to be restored, we must acknowledge our sin, thank God that Christ has paid our penalty, and reach out to accept God's forgiveness. The moment we do this, we experience the warm embrace of our Heavenly Father. The distance is gone. We are now walking in the light, having fellowship with God. "The blood of Jesus, his Son, purifies us from all sin" (1 John 1:7).

Before we go further, let's clarify the meaning of God's *forgiveness*. The psalmist says, "As far as the east is from the west, so far has he removed our transgressions from us" (Ps. 103:12). God's forgiveness is relieving the person from God's judgment—from the penalty due the sinner. Again the psalmist says, "He does not treat us as our sins deserve or repay us according to our iniquities" (Ps. 103:10). Isaiah the prophet spoke of God "blotting out" our sins and remembering them no more against us (Isa. 43:25). Clearly God's forgiveness means that our sins no longer stand as a barrier between us and God. Forgiveness removes the distance and allows us open fellowship with God.

"Forgiveness removes the distance and allows us open fellowship with God."—Gary Chapman

day Two

Confession, Repentance … and Forgiveness

Read Ephesians 4:32 in your Bible. What is our model for how we are to forgive others?

_____

In this divine model, there are two essential elements—confession and repentance on the part of the sinner and forgiveness on the part of the one sinned against. In the Scriptures, these two are never separated.

Two essential elements of forgiveness

1. Confession and repentance on the part of the sinner
2. Forgiveness on the part of the one sinned against

There is no scriptural evidence that God ever forgave anyone who did not repent of sin and turn in faith to Him. Some would object by raising the following question: What about Jesus' prayer on the cross, "Father, forgive them, for they do not know what they are doing" (Luke 23:34)? Was that prayer not answered by the Father? Yes, but not immediately. Not only were they not immediately forgiven, but they continued in the dastardly act of crucifying the Son of God.

That they were not forgiven immediately is clear from Peter's sermon recorded in Acts 2, which took place on the Day of Pentecost.

Read Acts 2:22-23. Peter was speaking to

_____

Read Acts 2:37-40. He pleaded with them to

_____

He was obviously preaching to some who actually participated in the crucifixion of Christ. More than three thousand responded to the truth and acknowledged Christ as Savior (v. 41). The rest of Acts records numerous others who responded to Christ. And in Acts 6:7 we read, "The number of disciples in Jerusalem increased rapidly, and a large number of priests became obedient to the faith." Apparently, it was after

Pentecost when many of those who crucified Jesus came to acknowledge Him as the Messiah and experienced God's forgiveness.

Jesus' prayer on the cross, "Father, forgive them, for they do not know what they are doing," is an indication of His willingness and deep desire that they experience the Father's forgiveness. It is this willingness to forgive that we must emulate. But those for whom He prayed did not experience the Father's forgiveness until they repented and placed their faith in Christ the Messiah.

day Three

Seeking Another's Repentance

Human forgiveness is to be modeled after divine forgiveness. Confession and repentance on the part of the one sinning and forgiveness on the part of the one sinned against are still the two essential elements to genuine reconciliation.

Let's look at the clear biblical paradigm Jesus laid out in Luke 17:3-4. Notice the progression of events. First, there is a sin committed—your brother, sister, or friend treats you unjustly. Immediately you experience valid righteous anger. Your first response is clear: You are to rebuke the person who sinned against you.

> "If your brother sins, rebuke him, and if he repents, forgive him. If he sins against you seven times in a day, and seven times comes back to you and says 'I repent,' forgive him" (Luke 17:3-4).

What is your response to the command to rebuke one who has sinned?
- ❑ **There is no way.**
- ❑ **I'd rather get over it on my own.**
- ❑ **Does that mean I can blast him?**
- ❑ **It's difficult, but I want to handle anger God's way.**

It is usually best to give yourself time to cool down emotionally before you make this rebuke. But to think that you are going to be totally calm when you have been sinned against in such a radical way is to be unrealistic. However, you must be careful not to sin in your rebuke.

You must exhibit Christian love in that your deepest desire is that the person will confess and repent of his wrong so that you may extend forgiveness. As Jesus was willing to forgive those who were putting Him to death, we, with the help of God's Holy Spirit, must be willing to forgive those who have caused us deep pain.

Next, the person who sinned must repent; that is, he must confess the wrong committed and express a desire to turn from practicing that wrong in the future.

According to Luke 17:3-4, if the person repents, what are you to do? _____

How many times? _____

We are to lift the penalty and receive the individual back into a restored relationship with us. And we begin the process of rebuilding trust. We refuse to allow someone's misdeed to keep us away, and we do not allow our feelings of hurt and disappointment to control our behavior. We forgive this person in the same manner God has forgiven us and in the same manner we hope He will forgive us if we sin against Him.

Forgiveness does not remove all the results of sin. When David sinned against Bathsheba and Bathsheba's husband, God fully forgave David when he confessed his sin. But the negative results of David's sin plagued him throughout the remainder of his life. The same is true of our sin. Forgiveness does not remove all the results of sin. We must be held accountable for our actions and we must seek to learn through our failures.

A second reality is that forgiveness does not remove all our painful emotions. Forgiveness is not a feeling; it is a commitment to accept the person in spite of what he or she has done. It is a decision not to demand justice but to show mercy. Nor does forgiveness mean we will never think of the situation again. Because every event in life is recorded in the brain, there is every potential that the event will return to the conscious mind again and again.

"Forgiveness is not a feeling; it is a commitment to accept the person in spite of what he or she has done."
—Gary Chapman

Have you chosen to forgive someone but still have memories of hurt feelings? ❑ **Yes** ❑ **No**

If you answered yes, spend time in prayer following these steps:

1. **Admit to God what you are thinking and feeling.**
2. **Thank Him that by His grace the offense is forgiven.**
3. **Ask Him for the power to do something kind and loving for that person.**

We can choose to focus on the future and not allow our minds to be obsessed with past failures that are now forgiven.

day *Four*

When the Person Doesn't Repent

Forgiveness, like communication, requires two parties. Forgiveness is a gift, one that cannot be opened until the sinner is willing to admit that "I need it and I want it."

There is no scriptural evidence that God ever forgives the unconfessing, unrepenting sinner. God is always willing to forgive, desirous of forgiving, but He cannot actually forgive until the sinner repents. The same is true in human relationships. Christians with the aid of the Holy Spirit must always stand ready to forgive, willing and desirous of forgiving, extending forgiveness, but we cannot force forgiveness to someone who does not desire it.

As you read Matthew 18:15-17 in the margin, underline the first thing you should do when someone wrongs you. Then complete the following:

The purpose of the confrontation is _____

_____

"If your brother sins against you, go and show him his fault, just between the two of you. If he listens to you, you have won your brother over. But if he will not listen, take one or two others along, so that 'every matter may be established by the testimony of two or three witnesses.' If he refuses to listen to them, tell it to the church; and if he refuses to listen even to the church, treat him as you would a pagan or a tax collector" (Matt. 18:15-17).

According to Galatians 6:1, the attitude of

confrontation is _____

_____

What then should Christians do with their angry feelings and thoughts when the persons who wronged them refuse to repent of the wrong committed? We are to lovingly confront the person as God confronts us. If the individual does not respond positively to our first confrontation, we are to pray for him and make another attempt, inviting one or two others to go with us, thus broadening the circle of knowledge about the sin. If the person does not respond in due time to this confrontation, then the reality of the sin must be shared with the larger community, which typically involves the extended family and in some cases, the church family. If the person still does not repent of the wrong, then he or she is to be treated as a "pagan." This is the word Jesus used. The Matthew 18 passage primarily addresses relationships between Christian believers, but the principle applies to all who let sin fracture a relationship. A pagan was an outsider, an unbeliever. Whether the offending person is an actual unbeliever or just an unrepentant Christian, we treat the individual the same, as one who has broken fellowship with us. We should continue to pray for him, to be kind to him, to treat him with dignity and respect. Remember, here is a person for whom Christ died, a person with whom we would desire to be reconciled. But we cannot act as though the sin does not exist. The sin has created a barrier between the two of you, and the barrier will not dissolve with time alone.

Read 2 Thessalonians 3:14-15. What is the purpose of disassociating from those who are unrepentant?
- ❏ **To make them pay for hurting you**
- ❏ **To emphasize they don't deserve to be around repentant people such as yourself**
- ❏ **To make them ashamed of their behavior so they'll repent and the relationship will be restored**

Two Decisive Steps

I believe the answer to dealing with one who doesn't repent lies in taking two steps. First, commit or release the person who has sinned against you to God. God alone knows everything about the other person, not only his actions but his motives. And God alone is judge. So the person who is eaten up with bitterness toward another who has treated him unfairly is to release that person to an all-knowing Heavenly Father who is fully capable of doing what is just and right toward that person.

God is in a far better position to be the judge than we. You can turn your erring friend and the wrong committed against you over to God, knowing that He will take the best possible action on your behalf. He is more concerned about righteousness than are you.

The second crucial step is for the person who has been sinned against to confess his own sin. Remember, anger itself is not sin, but often we allow anger to lead us to sinful behavior, such as an explosion or implosion. Thus angry employees returning to shoot it out with the supervisor are sinful; they are committing their own wrong and are compounding the problem. However, when we unleash verbal tirades against the person who has wronged us or if we commit acts of physical violence, we also are sinful. And let's not forget implosive anger: Anger held inside often becomes bitterness and hatred, both of which are condemned in Scripture as sinful.

As noted earlier in our study, anger was designed to be a visitor, never a resident. The biblical challenge is that we are to rid ourselves "of all such things as these: anger, rage, malice, slander, and filthy language" (Col. 3:8). When you or I become obsessed with our own hurt and anger, we are no longer focusing on God and are guilty of misguided passion. If ever there is a time when we need the help and guidance of God, it is when we have been wronged.

At that point, prayer is vital. The following prayer may help you take these two steps toward alleviating your own inner turmoil.

Father, You know the pain, the hurt, the anger, the bitterness that I feel toward _____. You know what he (she) has done to me. You know I have made every effort to seek reconciliation but he is unwilling to deal with the wrong. I recognize that I cannot make him do what I wish he would do. I commit _____ to You, knowing that You are a just and honest God. I put _____ in Your hands and trust You to work in his life what is best.

I also want to confess that I have allowed his wrong to consume me. I have become obsessed with my anger, my hurt, my disappointment, my frustration. I've had a bitter spirit toward this person and sometimes toward You for allowing this to happen. I want to confess that this is wrong, and I want to thank You that Christ has paid my penalty. I want to accept Your forgiveness for my wrong attitudes.

I pray that Your Spirit will fill my heart and my mind. I don't want my life to be ruined because of what the other person has done to me, and I know that is not Your desire. I want to follow You. I want to accomplish Your purposes. Let this be a day of new beginnings for me. In the name of Christ, my Savior and Lord. Amen.

Such a prayer, prayed sincerely, will channel the Christian's energies in the right direction, namely toward seeking God's fellowship and wisdom. If and when the other person confesses and repents of wrongdoing, we must stand ready to forgive and work at rebuilding the relationship.

ASKING FORGIVENESS FOR OUR SINS

This week we have talked primarily about our responsibility to confront family members and friends who sin against us and to seek reconciliation. However, there is another word from Jesus. It has to do with our own sin. His instructions are clear in Matthew 5:23-24.

When we sin against others, it is our responsibility to confess and repent of our own sins. We should take the initiative as soon as we realize we have done or said something unfairly to another. Whether I have sinned against someone else or someone has sinned against me, it is my responsibility to take the initiative to seek reconciliation. If I have sinned

"If you are offering your gift at the altar and there remember that your brother has something against you [that is, you have wronged him], leave your gift there in front of the altar. First go and be reconciled to your brother; then come and offer your gift" (Matt. 5:23-24).

against someone, very likely the person is experiencing anger toward me. If the person has sinned against me, then I am the one experiencing anger. Anger in God's economy is designed to motivate us to take constructive action in seeking to right the wrong and restore the fellowship with the other person.

Do you need to seek reconciliation from someone you have wronged? ❑ **Yes** ❑ **No**

How will you seek reconciliation this week? Write your action plan below.

_____

_____

_____

_____

_____

"Whether I have sinned against someone else or someone has sinned against me, it is my responsibility to take the initiative to seek reconciliation."
—Gary Chapman

leader Guide

To the Leader:

Do you have a broken relationship with a class member or another Bible study leader in your church? Prayerfully apply the principles you've learned in this week's study to seek reconciliation.

Before the Session

Enlist a volunteer to follow the instructions for the second option in Teaching Step 1.

During the Session

1. Invite participants to share a meaningful gift they have received and what made it so special. Guide the class to state the similarities between forgiveness and a physical gift. [Samples: can be offered, received or rejected; cost is involved; doesn't belong to the recipient until it is accepted.] OR Invite a volunteer to stand in front of the class. Direct the other participants to stand up and turn their backs to the volunteer. Instruct them to ignore the volunteer as he or she attempts to greet them. After a short time, ask everyone to be seated. Invite the volunteer to share how it felt being separated from the others. Ask other participants to share how they felt turning their backs to the volunteer and why.

2. Read Isaiah 59:2. Inquire: *Who is hurt by sin? Why?* Read Romans 6:23. Ask: *What is the ultimate separation from God? What gift did God offer so we could avoid this separation? How much did this gift of forgiveness cost?* Ask three volunteers to read Psalm 103:12; Isaiah 43:25; and Micah 7:19. Ask what word pictures these verses use to describe God's forgiveness.

3. Direct learners to complete just the "If" portion of the statement on page 59 to state what people must do to receive God's forgiveness. Discuss what it means to confess sins to God. Read Isaiah 59:12-13 as an example of confession. Then read Isaiah 59:20. Discuss what it means to "repent." Direct learners to complete the "Then" portion of the statement on page 59 to state what God will do when people acknowledge and turn from their sin.

4. Ask: *We're supposed to be studying how to process anger positively— why do we need to discuss and understand God's forgiveness?* Request that someone read Ephesians 4:31-32. Explain that instead of being angry with one another, God wants us to forgive one another.

Discuss the question at the beginning of Day 2. Ask the class to state the two essential elements in forgiveness. Ask: *Can there be forgiveness without repentance? Why?*

5. Invite someone to read Luke 17:3-4. Ask learners how they feel about rebuking someone and why. Comment: *We might rebuke a child or spouse, but should we rebuke a fellow church member or work colleague? If so, how?* Ask: *What must we do if the person we rebuke repents? In practical terms, what does it mean to forgive that person?* (If most participants are parents, discuss whether parents are supposed to lift penalties when they forgive their children and why.) Ask if participants have ever declared that they have forgiven someone but continued to feel hurt over the situation. Inquire: *Does that mean you didn't really forgive them? What does it mean? How did Dr. Chapman suggest we deal with our painful emotions?*

6. Ask a participant to read Matthew 18:15-17. Use the first activity of Day 4 (p. 63) to identify the purpose and attitude of confrontation. Direct the class to outline steps a believer should take when a person refuses to repent. Explain that the principle of taking one or two others along is based on the law's requirement in Deuteronomy 19:15 that no case be settled without two or three witnesses. Ask: *What if your spouse says something hurtful and doesn't repent—how can you follow these biblical commands without airing the family's dirty laundry in front of the whole church? Explain.* Discuss the final activity of Day 4. Ask: *Do we not have to forgive someone if he or she doesn't repent?* Explore how this disassociation is different from the withdrawal of implosive anger. Ask: *How can we apply this biblical teaching with family members without giving them the silent treatment?*

7. Guide learners to discuss the two steps they can take to process anger when the person who offended them refuses to repent. Explain that today's study has focused on believers' responsibilities when they have been wronged. Ask: *If we sin against someone, do we wait for him or her to confront us?* Read Matthew 5:23-24. Inquire: *What is the goal when any relationship has been disrupted by ours or someone else's sin?* Read Isaiah 1:18. Declare that God wants us to reason together with Him and one another so we can all enjoy the gift of forgiveness and unbroken relationships.

Processing Anger

day One

How God Feels Toward Our Anger

Christians often experience anger toward God in the face of tragedy. Often the stronger one's Christian commitment, the more intense will be the person's anger toward God. Job was "a righteous man" (see Job 1:8; 2:3). When God allowed Job to lose his wealth, his family, and his health, this righteous man felt intense anger toward God. Job said, "God has turned me over to evil men and thrown me into the clutches of the wicked." He lost his desire to live. "Only a few years will pass before I go on the journey of no return. My spirit is broken, my days are cut short, the grave awaits me. … My days have passed, my plans are shattered, and so are the desires of my heart" (Job 16:11,22; 17:1,11). Job did not understand why God would allow such tragedy into his life, and he was clearly angry with Him.

When we look at Job and other biblical examples of people who were angry with God, it is clear that God did not condemn such anger. Rather, He entered into conversation with these people and helped them work through their anger. However, this does not mean He always gave a full explanation of why bad things happened to good people.

After listening sympathetically to Job's expressions of anger toward Him, God's response was not one of condemnation. God reminded Job that His ways were not always understandable to men. He reminded Job that He is the all-powerful Creator and Sustainer of all that is and that in the final analysis, He is a God of justice who can be trusted (see Job 38–41). In the end, God expressed His own anger toward Job's friends for condemning him and urged them to repent of their wrongdoing and ask Job to pray for them. "My servant Job will pray for you, and I will accept his prayer and not deal with you according to your folly" (Job 42:8).

Job's ultimate response was to trust God even though he did not understand. Through this experience, Job's relationship with God deepened. In his own words, "My ears had heard of you but now my eyes have seen you." The Scriptures then record that "the Lord blessed the latter part of Job's life more than the first" (vv. 5,12).

"WHY DID GOD NOT DO SOMETHING?"

Describe a time you asked, "Why didn't God do something?" _____

_____

When I ponder this question, two alternatives come to mind, for clearly God *can* do something. One, God can eliminate all sinful people and thus wipe out all the pain caused by their sinful acts. This, however, would eliminate the entire human race, because the Bible says, "All have sinned" (Rom. 3:23). The second possibility would be for God to step in and miraculously avert the consequences of all evil. But apparently God values freedom, and freedom requires the option to disobey as well as to obey. There can be no freedom without the possibility of evil, and evil always has negative consequences.

In addition to the injustices caused by evil, Christians often struggle with the apparent personal inequities they endure. While the Bible tells us something of God's perspective, it does not reveal all of His plans.

Read the following Scriptures. Draw a line from the reference to the statement it makes about life's hardships.

John 9:1-3 — **Grief may be used to refine our faith.**

Romans 8:28-29 — **Our difficulties lead us to maturity.**

James 1:2-4 — **Our difficulties may be designed to display God's work.**

1 Peter 1:6-7 — **God works good out of everything and seeks to make us more like Christ through every experience.**

While all of these positive purposes are true, they still do not answer all the questions that race through our minds in the face of personal pain and loss. The call of God is that we will trust Him in the darkness as we trusted Him in the light. He has not changed.

> "The call of God is that we will trust Him in the darkness as we trusted Him in the light."
> —Gary Chapman

day Two

When You Are Angry Toward God

The problem with our anger toward God is not the anger itself but how we handle the anger. Your anger with God is distorted anger. God has done you no wrong, but what you feel is still real anger. In fact, your anger is not a choice. Anger was your response to a situation that brought great pain to you and that you believed God could have averted. Thus, in your mind, God has treated you unfairly. Anger is the normal human response when we encounter what we perceive to be injustice. God made us with the capacity for anger. However, what we do with our anger is our responsibility.

> "God made us with the capacity for anger. However, what we do with our anger is our responsibility."
> —Gary Chapman

The first step in responsibly handling our anger toward God is to *take the anger to God*. You can freely express your perception of things to God. He knows what you are experiencing and wants you to share your thoughts and feelings with Him. Biblical illustrations are abundantly clear that God does not condemn His children when they bring their anger to Him. Let's look at a couple of the examples we studied earlier.

> "God does not condemn His children when they bring their anger to Him."
> —Gary Chapman

The first mention of anger in the Bible is found in Genesis 4, where Cain experienced anger toward God because God accepted his brother Abel's sacrifice and did not accept his. God took the initiative to recognize and mention Cain's anger. Apparently, Cain would have tried to hide his anger from God. In taking the initiative, God clearly indicates that He wants us to talk with Him about our anger.

A second example is Jonah. He delivered his message of judgment: Forty days and God will destroy this city. The people of Ninevah repented; in response, God forgave them and lifted the judgment. Jonah's response to God's forgiveness was anger.

Read Jonah 4:1-3 in your Bible. Jonah's anger was negative, but what positive action did he take?

_____

Jonah shared his anger with God, telling Him specifically what he believed to be unfair. God was helping Jonah come to understand that his preaching was not an act of futility but was indeed successful and served the purposes God had intended.

These biblical illustrations indicate the value of talking to God about our anger. God is our compassionate Father and wants to hear our complaints. At the same time, He is also the sovereign God who does no wrong. He will either help us understand His perspective on our present situation or He will simply ask us to trust Him.

The second step in processing our anger with God is to *listen to God's message.* Having expressed our honest concerns to God, we are now in a position to listen to His "quiet whisper" to us. This sometimes comes through a trusted Christian friend or through a sermon by a faithful pastor. God's word may come through the words of an old hymn or a contemporary chorus, or it may come in your personal times of reading the Scriptures. Whenever God speaks, you will know it is His voice if the message you receive is consistent with Scripture. We listen to His voice, look for the good that may come out of this painful situation, and seek to grow in Christlikeness.

We must accept what has happened in our lives, choosing to believe that though we do not understand it, God will use it to accomplish His good purposes. Listening does not always lead to understanding, but it does lead to accepting our situation without malice toward God.

This stage of acceptance may come quickly or it may take weeks, even months. But for the believer who honestly shares his anger with God, eventually "the peace of God, which transcends all understanding" will settle upon the believer's heart and mind (Phil. 4:7).

After the peace of acceptance settles upon us, there is a third step in processing our anger toward God. We report for duty to *get our next assignment from God.* As long as we are alive, God is not through with us. You may be diseased, discouraged, disappointed, and in deep pain, but God has plans for us, and those plans are all good. As we get up and

Steps in responsibly handling anger:
1. Take the anger to God.
2. Listen to God's message.
3. Get your next assignment from God.

"Listening does not always lead to understanding, but it does lead to accepting our situation without malice toward God."
—Gary Chapman

begin to do what God has gifted us to do, it does not mean our pain has evaporated. It does mean our anger has been processed and is no longer a barrier between us and God.

For the Christian who learns to process his anger toward God constructively, the future holds hope in spite of the present pain. And for many believers, history will repeat the epithet of Job. "The Lord blessed the latter part of Job's life more than the first" (Job 42:12). We will receive God's blessing, and He will use us in great ways.

> "For the Christian who learns to process his anger toward God constructively, the future holds hope in spite of the present pain."
> —Gary Chapman

Fill in the blanks to review the steps to handling anger toward God.

1. Take _____ _____ to God.

2. _____ to God's message.

3. Get _____ _____ _____ from God.

If you are struggling with anger toward God right now, place a check beside the step you need to take next.

day Three

When You Are Angry at Yourself

As we have noted throughout this study, anger is an emotional and physical response of intense displeasure when we encounter someone or something we perceive to be wrong, unfair, or unjust. When we experience anger toward ourselves, it is because we perceive we are the ones guilty of the wrongdoing, the unkindness, the injustice, or the careless act.

The events that stimulate this self-focused anger may surface in any area of life. When we don't live up to our expectations, that is, we fail to accomplish what we know we are capable of doing in our vocation, hobbies, relationships, or church life, we may experience anger at ourselves.

Most of us sometimes act carelessly or foolishly. When these acts result in detrimental consequences, we tend to get angry with ourselves for being foolish or careless. Careless, thoughtless actions often create situations that stimulate self-focused anger.

Perhaps the area that brings the most intense anger to the Christian is when we violate our own strongly held values. The Christian husband who is sexually unfaithful to his wife may try to blame her for his "indiscretions" but may later experience intense personal anger for allowing himself to fall into immorality.

Any violation of one's moral values has the potential for eventually stimulating self-focused anger. The anger may come when the individual first realizes what he has done, or it may come when the wrongdoing is discovered by others and made public. As the individual begins to suffer the consequences of wrongdoing, his self-focused anger may arise.

Such anger is often accompanied by feelings of guilt. Anger and guilt should lead to repentance and refreshing forgiveness, which we will discuss later. However, sometimes we wallow in our guilt and turn our anger inward.

Briefly describe the last time you got angry at yourself.

_____

_____

Did you allow that anger to:
❑ **Overwhelm you with guilt and self-condemnation?**
❑ **Lead you to repentance and forgiveness?**

UNHEALTHY RESPONSES

Whatever the source of the anger we feel toward ourselves, we must learn to process it constructively. Two negative ways of expressing our anger are explosion and implosion, both of which we discussed earlier. These same destructive methods may be used in responding to the anger we feel toward ourselves. If we explode, then we give ourselves angry words and may treat ourselves with physical abuse. Our verbal explosions may be in private or in the presence of others, but we berate ourselves verbally. *"I can't believe I can be so stupid. I don't ever do anything right. How did I do this? I am so ashamed of myself. I don't think I can ever face the world*

If you have enjoyed these studies from Gary Chapman and desire to purchase your own copy of his book *The Other Side of Love* to read and study in greater detail, visit the LifeWay Christian Store serving you. Or you can order a copy by calling 1-800-233-1123.

again. I wish I could just die." Such verbal tirades may sometimes be accompanied by physical acts of violence. Pulling one's hair, scratching oneself, beating one's head against the wall or floor, cutting one's body with sharp instruments, and attempting suicide are all destructive ways of responding to anger toward oneself.

Implosion means that while we are not audibly expressing negative messages toward ourselves nor inflicting physical harm, we are attacking ourselves mentally and silently. On the outside we may appear to be calm but inside we are raging against ourselves. *I deserve to suffer; look what I did. I was so stupid. I don't know why anybody would believe in me again. I did what I knew was wrong. I don't deserve forgiveness.* Sometimes the thoughts are highly condemning. *My life is useless. I don't deserve to be happy. I don't have any reason to go on living.* These are the emotional mental records that play in the minds of those who internalize anger toward themselves. Such internal self-condemnation often has a detrimental effect on the body and brings on physical problems usually associated with the digestive and neurological systems of the body.

Read Psalm 38:4-8 in your Bible. How did the psalmist describe his guilt? _____

_____

Describe the physical and emotional problems he experienced. _____

_____

Obviously, neither explosion nor implosion are satisfactory ways to respond to one's anger toward self. How then must the Christian respond to this self-focused anger? We'll start talking about that tomorrow.

Healthy Responses to Anger

The following five steps represent healthy responses to your anger.

First, *admit your anger*. Admit it to yourself, to a trusted friend or family member, to a counselor or pastor, but admit that you are experiencing anger toward yourself. "I am really feeling angry at myself" is the first statement of healing. Admit the other thoughts and feelings that accompany your anger. Perhaps: "I feel so disappointed in myself. I feel so foolish or stupid for letting this happen. I feel like I have let people down, including myself and God. I feel so irresponsible." Express as clearly as you can what you are thinking and feeling.

If you like, write the statements down. Say them aloud to yourself and say them in prayer to God. But admit and declare your anger.

Read Psalm 51:3-4. If you had been David, angry with yourself after committing adultery, how would you have worded the prayer? Write your version below.

_____

_____

_____

Five Steps for Processing Anger:
1. Admit your anger.
2. Examine your anger.
3. Confess your wrongdoing to God and accept His forgiveness.
4. Choose to forgive yourself.
5. Focus on positive actions.

Second, *examine your anger*. Anger toward oneself may either be definitive anger or distorted anger. Definitive anger at yourself means that your anger grows out of an actual wrong you have committed. Distorted anger means that your anger has arisen from a perceived wrong rather than a real wrong. Both must be processed, but it is helpful to know the kind of anger you are dealing with. There is a vast difference between the anger a man feels when he hits his thumb with a hammer and the anger he feels when he has been sexually unfaithful to his wife. The latter is an immoral act, and the anger is definitive. On the other hand, hitting one's thumb with a hammer is not immoral.

Perhaps the man who hit his thumb with a hammer concludes that hitting his thumb was simply an accident; hammers and nail heads do not always attract each other, and the eye and the hand are not always coordinated. This man realizes that what he experienced is common to any person who has ever picked up a hammer. He really wasn't careless. His anger toward himself needs to be released and he needs to affirm his worth as a child of God who is imperfect and living in an imperfect world.

The husband who has been unfaithful to his wife has a much bigger issue with which to deal. He has broken one of God's clearly stated moral laws. He is feeling angry with himself, and his anger is definitive, rising from a moral wrong. With his anger he may feel guilt, shame, and embarrassment. All of these are normal and expected feelings when one has violated moral principles. He feels guilty because he is guilty; he feels shame because he did a shameful thing; he is embarrassed because others know about his sinful act. His anger at himself is real and must be processed, which brings us to the third step.

Third, *confess wrongdoing to God and accept His forgiveness*. There is only one appropriate way to process anger toward oneself that arises from one's own sin. We find that in 1 John 1:9. God loves us and wants to have fellowship with us, but because He is holy, our sin breaks that fellowship, and He must treat us as disobedient children. This means that He will rebuke and discipline us (see Heb. 12:5-11). But when we are willing to confess our sins, He is fully willing to forgive our sins. That is what the cross of Christ is all about. He took the punishment for our sins so that God could forgive us and still be just. Our part is to admit we need His forgiveness.

"If we confess our sins, he is faithful and just and will forgive us our sins and purify us from all unrighteousness" (1 John 1:9).

Read Psalm 51:7-9. Check the statement below that best indicates acceptance of God's forgiveness. Cleanse me and:
- ❏ **I'll try really hard to clean myself up as well.**
- ❏ **I'll beg for forgiveness every night anyway.**
- ❏ **I'll be clean.**

When our sin has been not only against ourselves and God but against another person, then we are to confess our wrongdoing to the person we sinned against and request his or her forgiveness. We empty our conscience of guilt toward God by confessing to God, and we empty our conscience toward man by confessing to the person we sinned against. True repentance of sin is always accompanied by a desire to admit our wrongdoing and make restitution to those against whom we have sinned. Confession is the first step in restitution.

Having experienced God's forgiveness and perhaps the forgiveness of the person we sinned against, we are now ready for step four.

Tomorrow we'll look at the final two steps in properly responding to personal anger.

day *Five*

More Healthy Responses to Anger

The fourth step in properly responding to personal anger is to *choose to forgive yourself*. Forgiving yourself is much like forgiving someone who has sinned against you. Forgiving someone else means that you choose to no longer hold the sin against that person. Forgiveness allows the two of you to communicate again, to listen to each other with a view to understanding. It opens up the potential of working together as a team.

At its root, self-forgiveness is a choice. You feel pained at your wrongdoing. You wish you had never sinned. The reality is that you have. Now it is time to forgive yourself. You must choose to do so. No positive purpose is served by berating yourself explosively or implosively. All such behavior is destructive and thus a sinful response to your anger. This too needs to be confessed to God.

Choosing to forgive yourself is best done in the context of prayer, letting God witness your self-forgiveness. The following prayer may help you express your thoughts and feelings to God.

Father, You know the wrong I committed. I have already confessed it to You, and I know You have forgiven it. Your Word says that You no longer remember that against me. I thank You for Your forgiveness. You also know that over the past few weeks I have put myself down, beaten myself with destructive words, told myself that I am not worthy of living, that I deserve to be punished forever, that I wish I could die. I know these self-destructive thoughts are not pleasing to You. Because You have given me life and because I have trusted in Jesus, I am Your child. I have no right to condemn myself after You have forgiven me. I confess these wrong attitudes to You, and I ask for Your forgiveness.

I thank You that You love me and that You freely forgive. Now understanding who I am—Your child—I forgive myself for the wrongs I have done. Even though the pain may follow me for a long time and when I think of my failures I may weep, I will no longer allow my past failures to keep me from doing the positive things You have called me to do.

With Your help, I remove those failures from my life forever and I commit myself to following You in the future.

Such a prayer, offered sincerely, can be the decisive step in forgiving yourself. Forgiveness releases you from the bondage of your past failures and gives you the freedom to make the most of the future. That brings us to step five.

Fifth, *focus on positive actions.* You are now in a position to change the course of your life. You can learn from your failures. Sometimes people make the mistake of trying never to think again about the failure. This, I believe, is a mistake. You can learn much from your failures. God wants to work good out of everything that happens to you (see Rom. 8:28). Your part is to cooperate with Him.

"Forgiveness releases you from the bondage of your past failures and give you the freedom to make the most of the future."
—Gary Chapman

Read Psalm 51:10-15. What positive actions did David take after he received forgiveness?

_____

_____

List positive actions you will take in response to what you have learned from a recent personal failure.

_____

_____

_____

To the Leader:

Contact participants who have been absent recently. Invite them to join you next week as you begin your study of Charles Stanley's *The Gift of Forgiveness.*

Before the Session

Be prepared to summarize Job 1 and 2 Samuel 11–12.

During the Session

1. Request participants recall a recent world or community tragedy. Ask: *What emotions were displayed? At whom was anger directed? Why might we get angry with God when tragedy strikes?* OR Relate: *Steve has worked hard for the same company for years but was passed over for a promotion two years ago. This year he felt he had a great chance for moving into a higher paying position. However, the day he was to interview for the position he overslept and then got caught in traffic. He was 30 minutes late for the interview and did not get the position.* Ask whom learners think Steve might be angry with and why.

2. Inquire whether learners agree with the first two statements of Day 1 and why. Lead a discussion with questions such as: *Is it a sin to be angry with God? Why? Is our anger toward God definitive or distorted? Explain.* Invite learners to respond to the first question in Day 1 (p. 72). Discuss Dr. Chapman's two alternatives to that question. Ask for volunteers to read the Scriptures listed in the second activity of Day 1. Discuss how those passages may answer the question, "Why didn't God do something?"

3. Admit that even though we know God is working through our trials we still may be angry He allowed those hardships. Ask learners to name the first step in responsibly handling our anger toward God. Briefly summarize Job 1. Organize the class into three groups. Direct Group 1 to read Job 7:11-21; Group 2 to read Job 10:1-9; Group 3 to read Job 30:20-27. Instruct groups to discuss: *How did Job take his anger to God? Does this passage make you uncomfortable? Why? How did Job still demonstrate faith even in his anger?* Ask the class: *Do you think there's a line you shouldn't cross when you take your anger to God? If so, what? How has God responded when you've expressed anger to Him?*

4. Ask what believers must do once they have voiced their complaints to God. Read Job 38:1-7 and 40:1-5. Ask: *Does God always give direct answers to your questions? What might God want to reveal to you instead? Why?* Request learners silently read Job 42:1-6 and state how Job responded to God's message. Invite participants to share how God's message has come to them and how they were able to hear it through their hurt. Read the quotation "Listening does not always lead to understanding, but it does lead to accepting our situation without malice toward God." Ask learners how they have discovered that to be true.

5. Guide participants to describe the third step in processing anger toward God. Talk about how positive action helps people make it through difficult times. Read Job 42:12,16-17. Invite volunteers to share how God has rewarded their faithfulness during trials.

6. Ask: *With whom do you most often get angry—family, strangers, God, or yourself? What are some reasons we get mad at ourselves? Are you easier or harder on yourself in your anger than you are on others? Why?* Request learners describe unhealthy responses to anger at oneself.

7. Ask the class to state the first step in responding positively to self-anger. Briefly relate the events of 2 Samuel 11:1–12:14. Explain that David wrote Psalm 51 after he was confronted by Nathan. Ask how David must have felt toward himself and why. Request someone read Psalm 51:1-4. Allow volunteers to share their responses to the first activity of Day 4 (p. 78). Ask the class to state the second and third healthy steps. Ask: *When is our anger against ourselves not valid? How can we process distorted anger when we really shouldn't be angry at ourselves and don't have any sin to confess?* Acknowledge that regardless of whether our anger is definitive or distorted, we still must forgive ourselves. Ask: *Is it harder to forgive yourself or others? Why? How do you forgive yourself? How can others help you? What makes forgiveness of yourself seem real?*

8. Ask for responses to the final activity of Day 5 (p. 81). Discuss positive actions learners have taken or can take to bring something good out of personal failures.

9. Invite volunteers to share the most helpful or challenging truths they've learned in this study.

Charles Stanley

is founder and president of In Touch Ministries, whose IN TOUCH radio and television program is broadcast around the world in 35 languages. He has also been senior pastor of the 15,000-member First Baptist Church in Atlanta, Georgia, for more than 30 years.

Dr. Stanley received his bachelor of arts degree from the University of Richmond, his bachelor of divinity degree from Southwestern Baptist Theological Seminary, and his master's and doctor's degrees from Luther Rice Seminary. He has twice been elected president of the Southern Baptist Convention and is the author of many books, including: *Finding Peace, God Is In Control, Seeking His Face, Walking Wisely, When Tragedy Strikes, The Source of My Strength, Success God's Way,* and *How to Listen to God.*

AMY SUMMERS wrote the personal learning activities and teaching plans for this study.

ABOUT THIS STUDY

**Read the Lord's Model Prayer in Matthew 6:9-13.
What two sides of forgiveness did Jesus teach us to pray about?**

_____

_____

Write a prayer, asking God to help you learn how to accept His complete forgiveness and to fully forgive others.

_____

_____

The Gift of Forgiveness

The following lessons flow from my struggle to forgive people whom I trusted and loved as my friends, yet they proved otherwise. More than anything, this book is simply an invitation to deal with the poison of an unforgiving spirit. It is a poison capable of ruining not only your life but the lives of those around you as well. It is my prayer that from these lessons you will discover the freedom that comes from putting behind you once and for all the hurts and injustices of yesterday.

Charles Stanley

Forgiveness and Freedom

day One

You've Got to Be Kidding!

"Forgive him? Are you kidding? After what he has done to me? I can *never* forgive him!"

"Forgive me? How could God forgive me? You don't know what I have done."

"How could I have done such an awful thing? I can never forgive myself."

These are the confessions I hear every day as a pastor. Confessions from people who have grown up in churches, grown up with godly parents, and yet grown up without ever fully understanding God's forgiveness and its intended effect on every level of their lives.

The tragedy of all this is the bondage people find themselves in when they do not grasp the immensity of God's forgiveness. It is a bondage that stifles their ability to love and accept those they know in their hearts most deserve their love. It is a bondage that cripples marriages from their outset. It is a bondage that is often passed from generation to generation. It is a bondage that chokes out the abundant life Christ promised to those who would believe.

Only by truly understanding God's forgiveness and making it a part of their lives will people be delivered from this bondage. Only then will they be able to enjoy the freedom that ensues and be able to live the Christian life to its fullest.

"How blessed is he whose transgression is forgiven, Whose sin is covered!" (Ps. 32:1).

Read Psalm 32:1 in the margin. What did David say was a source of blessing in life?

_____

How often do you experience blessing through giving and receiving forgiveness? (Circle one.)
Always   Usually   Sometimes   Never

WHAT IS FORGIVENESS?

Forgiveness is "the act of setting someone free from an obligation to you that is a result of a wrong done against you." For example, a debt is forgiven when you free your debtor of his obligation to pay back what he owes you.

Forgiveness, then, involves three elements: *injury*, *a debt* resulting from the injury, and a *cancellation of the debt*. All three elements are essential if forgiveness is to take place. Before we look in more detail at this process, however, we need to trace the sequence of events that lead to bondage when this process is abandoned. This is important because I believe most people who suffer from an unforgiving spirit do not know that unforgiveness is the root of their problem.

All they know is that they just "can't stand" to be around certain people. They find themselves wanting to strike out at people when certain subjects are discussed. They feel uncomfortable around certain personality types. They lose their temper over little things. They constantly struggle with guilt over sins committed in the past. They can't get away from the ambivalence of hating the ones they know they should love the most. Such feelings and behavior patterns often indicate that people have not come to grips with the forgiveness of God and the implications of that forgiveness.

Read Genesis 27:30-37,41 in your Bible and identify:

1. The injury inflicted on Esau _____

2. The debt resulting from that injury _____

3. Esau's response to the injury _____

TAKING HOSTAGES

We are all painfully aware of what it means for somebody to be taken hostage. We are outraged when the news of such an atrocity reaches us. And yet when we refuse to forgive others (or ourselves, for that matter), there is a sense in which we hold them hostage. Let me explain.

When a person is taken hostage on the international scene, the abductors usually want something; it may be money, weapons, or the release of prisoners. The message they send is, "If you give us what we want, we will give you back what we have taken." There is always some type of condition, a ransom of some sort.

When individuals refuse to forgive others for a wrong done to them, they are saying the same thing. But instead of holding people hostage until they get their demands, they withhold love, acceptance, respect, service, kindness, patience, or whatever the others value. The message they send is this: "Until I feel you have repaid me for the wrong done to me, you will not have my acceptance." If we go back to our definition, we can see that the element missing from this scenario is *cancellation of the debt*. Persons who refuse to forgive refuse to cancel the debt.

Read Genesis 33:1-4. How did Esau set himself and his brother free? _____

day Two

The Real Loser

A person who has an unforgiving spirit is always the real loser, much more so than the one against whom the grudge is held. This is easy to see when we take a closer look at the things most people withhold from those they feel have wronged them. Unforgiveness, by its very nature, prevents individuals from following through on many of the specifics of the Christian life and practically necessitates that they walk by the flesh rather than by the Spirit.

Think about your own experience for a moment. Think back to the last time someone really hurt you or wronged you or took something that belonged to you, whether it was a possession or an opportunity.

Immediately following the incident did you (circle one):
- **Feel like doing something kind for the person OR   Retaliating?**
- **Consider responding with gentleness   OR   Think about letting loose with well-chosen words?**

- **Feel like giving in and accepting the situation**
  OR   Fighting for your rights?

If you were honest, you probably identified more with the latter option in each case. These are the normal responses to being hurt or taken advantage of. But think of these responses in light of what Paul says in Galatians 5:22–25, and you will begin to understand why an improper response to injury automatically impairs a person's walk with God.

> **Read Galatians 5:22-25 in your Bible. List the fruit of the Spirit in the margin. Check the Christlike attributes you demonstrate when you have been wronged.**

In a broad sense Paul's list in Galatians 5:22–23 includes all the things we naturally want to hold hostage from the people who have hurt us. We rarely want to give our love to individuals who have hurt us. We certainly have no joy or peace when others have injured us in some way. We are not generally patient with or kind to people who have wronged us. We could go right down the list.

Paul accurately describes the responses of the unforgiving person in Galatians 5:19–21 in what he calls "the deeds of the flesh." An unforgiving spirit prevents a person from being able to walk consistently in the Spirit. The only choice is to walk according to the flesh. The consequences of such a life are devastating, and Paul discusses what will happen in Galatians 6:7–8:

> **Read Galatians 6:7-8 in your Bible and fill in the blanks. The logical consequence of harboring unforgiveness and walking in the flesh is_____.**
> **The result of forgiving and walking in the Spirit is**
> **_____ _____.**

The corruption Paul mentions has nothing to do with hell. He is talking about the consequences on this earth. If a person—believer or nonbeliever— makes decisions according to the impulses and desires of the flesh, the result will always be corruption—a wrecked and ruined life. Those persons who have not come to grips with the concept of forgiveness have by the very nature of unforgiveness set themselves up to walk according to the flesh. When that happens, they are losers every time. By withholding patience, kindness, gentleness, self-control, and the rest, the individual is held hostage by the flesh and, thus, is the ultimate loser.

A Consuming Corruption

The destructive nature of an unforgiving spirit is such that it is not limited to one relationship. Resentment and other negative feelings spill over into other relationships. This is the second reason a person with an unforgiving spirit loses out in life.

Unfortunately, people are rarely aware when hostility from one relationship affects their ability to get along with others. So they try and try—unsuccessfully—to work out their differences with others, never recognizing the real source of the problem. Once they tire of trying to change, they excuse their insensitivity as part of their personality and expect people to "work around" them, emotionally speaking. They develop a take-me-or-leave-me-but-don't-try-to-change-me attitude, and in the process they hurt people they love the most.

THE REJECTION CONNECTION

The third reason a person with an unforgiving spirit loses out in life is closely tied to the other reasons we've just discussed. When a person is wronged in some way, whether in marriage, business, friendship, or some other relationship, rejection occurs. The classic case would be when a guy breaks up with his girlfriend because he found another girl. In her struggle with rejection the girl swears she will never trust another male.

It is easy to see where hurt resulted from rejection. But if we plug this concept into other sets of circumstances, we can see it holds true in every case where forgiveness is needed.

An incident set my son and me at odds for years and illustrates how an unforgiving spirit has feelings of rejection at its roots.

When Andy was about 14, he discovered he had some musical talent. He began spending a great deal of time playing the piano, primarily by ear. That meant a great deal of pounding chords with very little melody. To me, it sounded all the same.

One day on my way upstairs I stuck my head in the living room and said, "Andy, is that all you know?" To my uninformed ear, it sounded as if he had been playing the same song for hours! He immediately stopped playing. And he never played for me again. He would wait until my wife and I left the house, and then he would spend hours practicing and practicing. I began hearing from others what a fine pianist Andy was, but I never heard another sound from the piano in the living room.

Some years later—when Andy was in his twenties—our conversation turned toward his music. He gave me his version of what happened in the living room that afternoon, and he confessed that he had resented me from that day on. Why? It really was not a big deal to me. I did not mean anything serious by what I said. But to Andy, as a teenager, what I communicated was this: "I do not accept you or your music."

He was too young to understand that my comment was directed at his music, not at *him* as my son. And I was too insensitive to understand that the budding young artist saw little distinction between his work and his personhood. And so I crushed him, and he held it against me. By Andy's own admission, the resentment he held in his heart toward me spilled over into other relationships in his life, primarily those having to do with authority.

What I want you to understand is that the cause of his resentment was perceived rejection. I say "perceived" because I did not intend to reject him. His response, however, was the same as if it had been intentional.

> **Consider an event in your life when you were hurt by rejection. As you look back on that situation now, would you say:**
> ❑ **The offending person intentionally meant to hurt or reject you?**
> ❑ **You misunderstood the situation and perceived the rejection?**

LOST AND FOUND

After years of listening to people recount how they have been hurt and mistreated by parents, spouses, kids, employers, and even pastors, I am convinced that at the beginning of each story is an experience that has been interpreted as rejection. As the rejection evolves into an unforgiving spirit, and eventually into bitterness, it takes a terrible toll. The person is left with a deep sense of emptiness, an inner sense that something is missing. Consequently, the individual seeks to regain what has been lost—and almost always in the context of relationships that are unrelated. Some people will go to almost any extreme to find what they have lost through intentional or unintentional rejection. People harboring unresolved resentment can feel driven to explore all kinds of avenues—usually ones that are not in keeping with the Christian life.

Read 2 Timothy 4:9-18 in your Bible.
How did Paul experience rejection? _____
Record the phrase that demonstrates he responded with forgiveness. _____
What empowered Paul to cancel the debt of those who harmed him? _____

day Four

The Waiting Game

There is a fourth reason an unforgiving spirit can devastate a life. Since the person with the unforgiving spirit is usually waiting for the other person to make restitution, a great deal of time may go by. During this time, fleshly patterns of behavior and incorrect thought processes develop. As I mentioned before, other relationships are damaged. Even after an unforgiving spirit is corrected, the side effects can take years to deal with, especially in the area of relationships.

The irony of the situation is this: By refusing to forgive and by waiting for restitution to be made, individuals allow their personal growth and development to hinge on the decision of others they dislike to begin with. They allow themselves to be held hostage. They say, "If he apologizes." "If she comes back to me." "If he rehires me." "If they invite me." They play the game of waiting for others to make the first move. In the meantime they allow an unforgiving spirit to weave its way into the total fabric of their lives.

Read Matthew 5:23-24 and 18:15 in the margin. Who is to make the first move toward reconciliation when:
You have sinned against someone else? _____
Someone else has sinned against you? _____

"Therefore if you are presenting your offering at the altar, and there remember that your brother has something against you, leave your offering there before the altar and go; first be reconciled to your brother, and then come and present your offering" (Matt. 5:23-24).

"If your brother sins, go and show him his fault in private; if he listens to you, you have won your brother" (Matt. 18:15).

Another ironic element is that sometimes the person who has done the wrong has no idea anything is wrong. A senior in the high-school department of our church had a good relationship with my son, who was serving as youth pastor at the time. Andy began to notice that Kim was not as friendly as she had been and that she became less and less involved in the youth department. He would make a point to speak to her, but his kindness was rarely returned.

After several months went by, he took the youth skiing. It so happened that late one evening on the trip Kim approached Andy and said she needed to talk. She began by apologizing for her attitude. She admitted she had been hurt by Andy and she had been holding something he said to her against him for some time. Then she asked him if he knew what he had said that hurt her so badly. Andy thought and thought and came up with nothing.

She looked surprised, reprimanded him for his insensitivity, and said, "Several months ago I spoke to you in Sunday School and told you our family had just bought a new pet."

Andy still drew a blank.

She continued, "You asked me what we got, and I told you it was a bird. Do you remember what you said then?"

At that point Andy remembered the conversation as well as his response to the news that her family had acquired a bird. "Yes," he said, "I do remember. I told you birds were messy and asked why you didn't get something more useful like a dog."

Andy immediately apologized, and his friendship with Kim was restored. Unfortunately, months were wasted because she would not deal with her hurt, and he did not know he had done anything.

A great deal of the hurt and rejection we face is unintentional. The seeming lack of concern on the part of those who hurt us is often not an attempt on their part to be insensitive.

Read Ecclesiastes 7:20-22 in your Bible. In the statements below, fill in the blanks with names of those you either need to forgive or seek forgiveness from.

1. Nobody is perfect. I forgive _____ for hurting me, either unintentionally or intentionally.

2. I need to quit being so sensitive. I forgive _____ for what he or she said to me. I realize now that _____ may have meant nothing by it.

3. I hurt others by my words too. I will go and seek forgiveness from _____ for what I said.

Some Choose to Lose

From what we've examined in this lesson, I hope you clearly understand this: *A person who harbors unforgiveness always loses.* Regardless of how wrong the other person may have been, refusing to forgive means reaping corruption in life. And that corruption begins in one relationship, including the relationship with God, and works its way into all the rest.

Holding on to hurt is like grabbing a rattlesnake by the tail; you are going to be bitten. As the poison of bitterness works its way through the many facets of your personality, death will occur—death that is more far-reaching than your physical death, for it has the potential to destroy those around you as well.

Read James 3:14-18 in your Bible. Use the chart to contrast a bitter person with one who forgives.

A Bitter Person	A Wise, Forgiving Person

MAKING THE PLUNGE

Have you been hurt? Has somebody, somewhere in your past, rejected you in such a way that you still hurt when you think about it? Do you become critical of people in your past the minute their names are mentioned? Did you leave home as a child or a college student with great relief that you were leaving, swearing you would never return?

Have you worked hard all your life not to become like your parents? Are there people in your past upon whom you would enjoy taking revenge? Have you made a pastime out of scheming about how you could get back at them or embarrass them publicly? Were you abused as a child? Maybe even molested? Did you suffer through your parents' divorce as a child? Were your parents taken from you when you were very young?

Were you forced by circumstances to pursue a different career from the one you originally wanted to pursue? Were you unable to attend the school of your choice because of financial reasons? Were you pushed out of a job opportunity by a greedy friend? Were you promised things by your employer that never came about?

If you answered yes to any of these questions, you may be on the brink of being set free from a bondage that you did not even know was keeping you a victim. You may be about to understand for the first time why you act the way you do in certain circumstances and why you cannot seem to control your temper. You may be on the verge of receiving the God-given insight you need to restore your war-torn home—this time for good.

Whatever your situation, whatever has happened in your past, remember that you are the loser if you do not deal with an unforgiving spirit. And the people around you suffer too.

I am writing so that you may be set free. In the process you may experience some pain. In some instances, it may be pain you have worked for years to avoid. Yet that pain is necessary for healing to take place.

It is my prayer that you will read and study each lesson carefully and prayerfully. It is my goal to bring old truths to bear on the damaging experiences of your life. And in doing so, I hope to give the Holy Spirit an opportunity to make you whole.

Read John 8:32 in your Bible and complete this statement: If I will hear, accept, and obey the biblical truths about forgiveness from this study, I will be

_____.

NOTES

leader Guide

Before the Session

Be prepared to relate the story of Joseph found in Genesis 37–45.

During the Session

1. State: *A drunk driver kills your child. Your spouse has an affair. Your business partner stabs you in the back and leaves you bankrupt. A family member molests a child.* Ask: *Which of these are unforgivable? Which would you have the hardest time forgiving? What would you accomplish by not forgiving?*

OR

Lead a discussion about types of "security blankets" participants had when they were children, how long they kept that item, and what it did for them. Ask how people might cling to unforgiveness as a type of security blanket. Ask: *What do they hope unforgiveness will do for them? What will it really do?*

2. Remark that in the last six lessons on anger you discovered a positive response to anger involves choosing to forgive. These next seven lessons will lead you into a deeper look at the gift of forgiveness. Comment that regardless of how hard it is to forgive someone, choosing not to forgive is far more painful. Forgiveness is the only route to peace and freedom.

3. Ask what Dr. Stanley stated occurs when forgiveness is not accepted or offered. Request someone read Psalm 32:1. Discuss: *What blessings have you received because you have been forgiven? How have you been blessed by forgiving others?* Request someone read the definition of *forgiveness* from Day 1. Ask participants to identify the three elements involved in forgiveness. Discuss the two activities about Jacob and Esau in Day 1. Invite volunteers to recall the story of Joseph and identify the injury done to him and the resulting debt. (Or, be prepared to tell Joseph's story in your own words.) Invite someone to read Genesis 45:4-5,14-15. Ask: *Would you have faulted Joseph for remaining angry with his brothers? What would he have accomplished by not forgiving them? What resulted from his cancellation of their debt?*

4. Discuss how Dr. Stanley equated unforgiveness with taking hostages. Ask participants to identify from Galatians 5:22-23 what we may withhold from people who have hurt us. Inquire: *When we choose to withhold these from others, who really becomes the hostage? According to Galatians 5:19, what holds us hostage?* Discuss the last activity of Day 2. Explain the meaning of "corruption" for the believer. Ask: *Following Dr. Stanley's line of reasoning in Day 2, why is the person with an unforgiving spirit always the loser?* Read Galatians 5:25. Remark that a person is set free from the destructive deeds of the flesh by choosing to walk in the Spirit.

5. Request participants identify from Day 3 the second reason why an unforgiving person loses out in life. Allow participants to describe how they have observed unforgiveness toward one person spill over into other relationships. Ask participants if they agree that an unforgiving spirit is often rooted in feelings of rejection, and why. Recount the story of Charles and Andy Stanley. Ask: *Are you more likely to say something flippantly not aware of how it might hurt, or are you more likely to perceive rejection from an innocent remark?* Ask how both Dr. Stanley's actions and Andy's response present challenges to a believer. Ask someone to read Ecclesiastes 7:20-22. Discuss how the common-sense principles from this passage can help believers choose to forgive when they feel rejected.

6. Ask someone to identify from Day 4 the fourth reason an unforgiving spirit leads to a losing life. Lead the class to describe the "waiting game" of forgiveness. Discuss the first activity of Day 4. Remind the class you discussed the importance of taking the initiative in seeking reconciliation in week 5 of their study of *The Other Side of Love*.

7. Acknowledge that some people who have harmed us may never repent or even feel sorry. Ask: *Does their lack of remorse mean you can never forgive? Who determines whether or not you can forgive a person and cancel that person's debt against you? Who is really hurt when you refuse to forgive?* Discuss the first activity of Day 5. Declare that the purpose of this study is to help people find freedom from bitterness so they can experience the blessings of forgiveness. Close in prayer, asking that that purpose will be achieved in each participant's life.

The Big Picture

day One

Attitudes are difficult things to change. I can remember as a child being told to "change my attitude," as if there were some button I could push that would instantly cause something to happen inside my head! In dealing with an unforgiving spirit—or a grudge as some call it—people need a big change in attitude. Attitudes change when we get all the facts, when we see the big picture. In this lesson we will be taking a look at the big picture concerning forgiveness. We will be gathering facts that will give us the perspective we need to understand the basis of God's forgiveness.

Sin Creates a Deficit

Sin creates a deficit in God's economy. Whenever there is sin, something is taken or demanded from the sinner. In Genesis 3 the serpent lost its standing in the animal kingdom because of its part in the temptation of Adam and Eve (v. 14). Adam and Eve lost the perfect harmony that once characterized their relationship (v. 16). Adam and Eve lost their home in the garden of Eden (v. 24).

> **Read Genesis 4:10-14 in your Bible. What did Cain lose as a result of his sin?** _____
>
> **Have you ever lost your place to belong or the ability to work effectively because of your sin? If so, describe briefly.** _____
>
> _____

We could go right through the Scriptures illustrating this principle. Whenever there is sin, the sinner loses something that is outside the sinner's power to regain.

Another principle, however, runs parallel with this one. Historically, whenever human beings sin against God, He provides a channel through which fellowship can be reestablished and maintained. This is an important concept as we look into the idea of forgiveness because we see in it God's desire to have fellowship with sinful, disobedient men and women.

This principle demonstrates God's willingness to give the human race a second chance. All of history is the outworking of God's strategy to bring humankind back into fellowship. The groundwork for your forgiveness and mine was laid immediately after the first sin was committed, and God has been building on that foundation ever since.

As I stated, sin creates a deficit in God's economy. Whenever there is sin, something is taken or demanded from the sinner.

> **Read Genesis 2:16-17 in your Bible. What did God warn would be taken from Adam and Eve as a result of their sin?** _____

What God ultimately requires of the sinner as a result of the sin is death—the death of the sinner. And we find in Revelation 20:15 that this death entails more than the giving up of physical life. It means eternal separation from God.

If you desire to dig deeper...

What was lost as a result of sin in the following passages?

1 Samuel 2:27-33:

_____

1 Samuel 15:17-29:

_____

2 Samuel 12:7-14:

_____

"And if anyone's name was not found written in the book of life, he was thrown into the lake of fire" (Rev. 20:15).

day Two

What's the Holdup?

So some questions arise: If the penalty for sin is death, why did God not immediately snuff out the lives of Adam and Eve? Did He not say that on the "day" they sinned they would "surely die"? Why does He not do the same for all sinners? What is He waiting for? Why did He provide Cain and Abel and later Israel with a system through which fellowship could be restored if sin ultimately resulted in death?

The answer is simple yet life-changing in its profundity. There is something God wants more than retribution. There is something He desires more than simply being paid back for the disrespect shown Him. God wants fellowship with us. And He was willing to put His own system of justice on hold while He made provision for sinful men and women to be rescued.

IS THERE ANY DOUBT?

Consider this crucial question: Do you realize that the God of the universe desires to have fellowship with you? You may say, "But you don't know what I've done!" I know this. Whatever you have done pales into insignificance beside the sin of Adam and Eve.

> **Read the following verses in your Bible and note how Adam and Eve's sin affected:**
> **The entire creation (Gen. 3:17):** _____
> **The entire human race (Rom. 5:12):** _____

Their sin made death a reality for all that breathes, both human and animal. But if God was willing to move so quickly to restore fellowship with Adam and Eve, does it make sense that He would move any less quickly to restore fellowship with us?

The big picture is simply this: People turned their backs on God and God immediately went to work to regain fellowship. These observations should be enough to convince us that God is a God of love and forgiveness. He forgives because He desires to forgive, not because He is under some constraint. His forgiveness is not handed out on an individual basis depending on the sin committed.

HIS WAY OR YOUR WAY?

A major hindrance to our ability to experience God's forgiveness is our unwillingness to accept God's frame of reference concerning sin and our inability to do anything about it. Instead, some people create for themselves a procedure for finding forgiveness and impose it upon God. In time their emotions become so attuned to their own way of thinking that it is almost impossible for them to accept any other way. Usually, their alternate systems underestimate the consequences of sin and overestimate their ability to remedy the situation.

You may be one of these people. I urge you to think about two things. First, God and God alone fully understands the reality of your sinful condition. Only God understands your need in terms of your relationship with Him. Therefore, regardless of what your mind and emotions may tell you, regardless of what may seem fair or unfair, God's plan for forgiveness is the only plan in which you can put your trust with any assurance.

Second, since that is true, are you willing to examine your heart and ask God to reveal any alternative systems you may have been clinging to? ❏ **Yes** ❏ **No**

Are you willing to lay aside those things and ask God to show you His way to true forgiveness? ❏ **Yes** ❏ **No**

If you answered yes, spend time in prayer about these matters now.

Cain decided to approach God his way, according to what made sense to him. The result of his decision was disastrous. If you insist on seeking forgiveness any way but God's way, the result will be no less disastrous for you. But if you look at your sin and God's provision for dealing with it from His perspective, you will experience freedom that comes with knowing *you are truly forgiven*!

day Three

The Bottom Line

The bottom line is that through Christ, God did away with the problem of sin insofar as its ability to keep us from having a relationship with Him. Let's examine how He did that.

The entrance of sin into the world meant that members of the human race lost physical life (a gradual process) and righteous standing before God. Fellowship with the sinless Creator was interrupted. But there was another angle to sin and its relationship to death. God demanded the life of the sinner: "For the wages of sin is death" (Rom. 6:23). Sin earned the sinner death. Although sin deserved immediate action on God's part, God in His mercy did not immediately judge humankind. He chose to suspend judgment to give His people a second chance. Thus He established a temporary system through which fellowship could be restored and

If you desire to dig deeper...

Record characteristics of God named in the following verses.

Exodus 34:6

_____

Leviticus 19:2

_____

Deuteronomy 32:4

_____

Malachi 3:6

_____

Romans 2:11

_____

maintained and sin could be covered—but not forgiven. Sin would have to be forgiven before the problem of sin could be solved once and for all. That is where Christ entered the picture.

Read Hebrews 9:13-14 in your Bible and fill in the blanks.

God's temporary system involved the _____ of _____ and cleaned _____.

God's permanent solution for sin involved the _____ of _____ and cleans _____.

GOD'S NATURE

To understand how the coming of Christ facilitated the forgiveness of sin, we must understand some basics about the nature of God. God's righteousness, that is, His sinlessness and holiness, by definition set up a standard that all those who would have fellowship with Him must meet. To put it another way, certain things must be true about people to be acceptable to God.

When I say this standard is set up by definition of His righteous nature, I mean that God did not arbitrarily establish this standard as we would establish the rules of a game. If that were the case, He could just change His standard and everybody would be acceptable. God's righteous standard flows from His unalterable nature. God's nature demands that certain things be true of those who desire to have uninterrupted fellowship with Him and who desire to someday dwell in His very presence. Specifically, His nature demands sinlessness, or perfection, but the presence of sin makes us unacceptable to Him.

Read Isaiah 59:1-2 in your Bible and Romans 3:23 from the margin. What has come up short?
❑ **God's ability to save you**
❑ **Your ability to attain God's standards**

"For all have sinned and fall short of the glory of God" (Rom. 3:23).

Our sin causes us to "fall short." Our sin disqualifies us in light of God's standard. Sin puts us in a relationship with God wherein we owe Him something. We must pay for what we have done much like common criminals must repay society for the crimes committed. Thus, the solution must in some way remove the consequences of our sin and restore us to a state in which our sin is no longer counted against us. Somehow, what was done through sin must be undone. So, how can that happen? How can the sinful be made the sinless?

Pardon and Payment

Like persons convicted of a felony, we lost our citizenship. Sin resulted in the forfeiture of our right to enter the kingdom of God. Like a governor, God has the power to pardon those who are guilty. There is one major difference, though. In our system of law a crime does not have to be paid for. A governor can pardon a convicted person, and that is the end of it. But the nature of God requires that those who dwell in His presence must be sinless, which means we must have committed no sins or have no sin that has not been paid for. God's nature will not allow Him to simply overlook sin. Sin carries with it a penalty that must be paid.

Read Hebrews 9:22 in your Bible.
What is the only thing that will pay sin's penalty?

_____

Think of it like this. A builder cannot make the payments on his bank loan. He goes to the president of the bank and apologizes for being so irresponsible. He asks the president to forgive him and then expresses an interest in doing business with the bank in the future. Regardless of how kind and understanding the president of the bank is, the nature of his job restricts him from simply patting the builder on the back and saying, "No hard feelings. We understand. Forget about the money and try to be more careful next time." It does not work that way. The builder will not be in good standing with the bank until his debt is paid.

Our sin and the debt that resulted left us in a position wherein we needed both *pardon* and *payment*.

BAD NEWS/GOOD NEWS

You will notice that neither the *degree* of sin nor the *quantity* of sin has been mentioned. That is because both are irrelevant. Yet if you are like many people I talk to every week, these are the two issues you may be wrestling with as you question God's willingness or ability to forgive you. It took only one less-than-perfect move to forfeit the right to a relationship with God. That is the bad news. The good news is that there are no degrees of separation.

Perhaps this example will clarify what I mean. Two people lost their jobs. One was fired for coming in to work late, the other for stealing from the cash register and falsifying his time card. What the first guy did was not even in the same league with the actions of the second. But fired is fired, and neither had a job.

If you can understand that everyone is in the same boat in terms of separation from God, it will be far easier for you to accept God's solution to the sin problem.

> **Read Romans 5:18 in your Bible. Into what two categories did Paul place every person? (Circle one each.)**
>
> • **Occasional sinner OR Habitual sinner**
> • **Breaker of minor laws OR Breaker of major laws**
> • **Justified OR Condemned**

PAID IN FULL

Using the analogy of indebtedness when talking about sin and its consequences fits perfectly with the New Testament's approach to the subject. Read what Paul writes in Colossians 2:13–14.

Paul's use of the word *having* implies the idea of means. Forgiveness is the way in which God makes us alive. The phrase "having forgiven us all our transgressions" means the same thing as "having canceled out the certificate of debt consisting of decrees against us." Forgiveness, then, is the cancellation of a debt. Paul is referring to a practice familiar to his first-century audience. In those days a man who owed another man would write out a *certificate of debt*. The certificate would include all that was owed along with the terms of payment. The debtor, the lender, and a witness would sign the document.

In a sense each of us had a certificate of debt against us, and Christ's death canceled the certificate. Paul says, "He has taken it out of the way, having nailed it to the cross." Often an ex-debtor would nail up his canceled certificate of debt in a public place so all would know his debt had been paid. Paul picks up on this practice and says that our debt was nailed to the cross with Christ, signifying that it had been paid in full: It was no longer legally binding.

Based on Paul's analogy, there should be no question that total forgiveness of sin comes through Christ. And that includes all sins—the ones we have already committed and the ones we will commit. From the perspective of the cross, they were all future. And it was from that perspective they were dealt with. So Paul could say to believers he had never met, "He made you alive together with Him, having forgiven us all our transgressions" (Col. 2:13). Paul did not need to know how many sins the Colossian believers had committed. He did not need to know the nature of their sins. All he needed to know was that they had approached God for forgiveness through Christ. That was enough then—and that is enough for us today!

I can say to you, with perfect assurance, that if you have trusted Christ's death on the cross to be the payment for your sins, your sins are forgiven. No matter what you have done, how many times you have done it, or who you hurt in the process, God has forgiven you.

If doubts about your particular situation remain in your mind, it should be obvious that you are still thinking about forgiveness according to your own artificial standards. The guilt you continue to carry around because of past sins is unnecessary. Now you must accept the truth about your past hopelessness as well as your present forgiven state: *You are forgiven.*

Read from the margin what Paul wrote in Colossians 2:13-14.

"When you were dead in your transgressions and the uncircumcision of your flesh, He made you alive together with Him, having forgiven us all our transgressions, having canceled out the certificate of debt consisting of decrees against us, which was hostile to us; and He has taken it out of the way, having nailed it to the cross" (Col. 2:13-14).

"My God, My God"

"When the sixth hour came, darkness fell over the whole land until the ninth hour. At the ninth hour Jesus cried out with a loud voice, 'ELOI, ELOI, LAMA SABACHTHANI?' which is translated, 'MY GOD, MY GOD, WHY HAVE YOU FORSAKEN ME?' " (Mark 15:33-34).

At this point you may be asking, "If our sin demanded a death—but this death involved eternal separation from God—how could Christ pay the penalty for our sin and still sit at the Father's right hand? If He took our place, it would seem He should go to hell. That is where we were heading, wasn't it?" In searching for answers, we are once again confronted with God's insatiable desire to restore fellowship with humankind. Christ did have to suffer the punishment we would have had to suffer. Mark 15:33–34 describes the events surrounding the crucifixion of Jesus.

While hanging on the cross, Christ experienced for our sake separation from His Heavenly Father. The separation was so deep that Christ even addressed Him differently. Until that time He had spoken of God as His Father. All of a sudden He cried out, "My God." There was no longer the intimacy, the warmth, or the closeness. Why the change? Because sin required separation from the Sinless One. In taking on the responsibility of our sin, Christ voluntarily put Himself in a position in which He no longer had fellowship with the Heavenly Father.

Read Hebrews 10:12-14 in your Bible. Where did Jesus go after suffering the punishment for our sins?

_____

Christ was accepted back into fellowship with His Heavenly Father based upon His own righteousness. He needed no sacrifice for His sin. He had no debt that needed paying, because He was sinless. He had the right through His own merit to sit at the right hand of God.

TAKE IT OR LEAVE IT

There we have it. Christ is God's solution for dealing with sin. Only through Christ can we find forgiveness. But once it has been found, it is a settled issue—past sin, present sin, and future sin. The details of what we have done, why we did it, and how many times we did it are irrelevant. Sin is sin; lost is lost; paid is paid; forgiven is forgiven. Either we have it or we don't.

Are there sins from your past that continue to hang over you like a dark cloud? ❑ Yes ❑ No

When you pray, does something inside you cause you to doubt that God is going to listen because of your past? ❑ Yes ❑ No

Do you feel that your potential for the kingdom of God has been destroyed because of your past disobedience? ❑ Yes ❑ No

If you answered yes to any of these questions, you have not yet come to grips with God's solution to your sin. You are still holding on to a way of thinking that will keep you in bondage the rest of your life. You have set yourself up to live a defeated life in which you will never know your potential for the kingdom of God.

I want you to be free. More important, God wants you to be free. And because He does, He sacrificed what was dearest to Him. Not until you are able to see yourself as a forgiven child of God will you begin to enjoy the fellowship that the death of His Son made possible.

leader Guide

To the Leader:

Conduct your own personal study of Leviticus 16 and Hebrews 9–10 to gain a basic understanding of the Old Testament sacrificial system and how it was merely a copy of the real sacrifice Christ would make on the cross. You don't need to present all this information to the class, but your background knowledge needs to support the class discussion of these passages.

Before the Session

Discover the current federal deficit at *www.publicdebt.treas.gov.* Click "public debt" at the top of the page; then click "Daily Amount to the Penny."

During the Session

1. Read this quotation from A. W. Tozer: "*I believe that the chronic unhappiness of most Christians may be attributed to a gnawing uneasiness lest God has not fully forgiven them, or the fear that He expects as the price of His forgiveness some sort of emotional penance which they have not furnished.*"[1] Ask participants why they agree or disagree with that statement. Comment that if believers are to get rid of an unforgiving spirit, they must recognize that God has forgiven them fully and there is no penance they can pay to earn forgiveness.

   OR

   Write 7,869,521,621,947.05 on the board (or the current deficit you obtained online). Ask participants to guess what that number signifies. [Federal deficit as of August 2005 or the current deficit.] Declare each citizen's share of that debt is around $30,000.[2] Discuss what participants think created the deficit and whether they think the U.S. will ever pay off its debt. Ask if participants are able to pay their portion of the debt. Comment that sin creates a deficit in God's economy that is even more impossible to pay off than the federal debt. It takes an act of God to erase that sin debt.

2. From the first activity of Day 1 discuss what Cain lost because of sin. Read some or all of the Scriptures in the "Dig Deeper" activity in the margin and discuss what was lost in each instance. Encourage participants to share how they have observed how people have lost some of the same things (job, family, home) because of sin. Ask what the ultimate payment for sin is and discuss what kind of death the Scriptures are referring to.

3. Invite volunteers to read the Scriptures in the "Dig Deeper" activity in the margin of Day 3. Ask participants to name qualities of God

from each verse. Record responses on the board. Ask which aspects of God's nature means He must require a payment for sin and which aspects lead God to hold off on His punishment. Ask what God wants more than retribution for sin. [fellowship]

4. Write *God* and *Humanity* on opposite sides of a writing surface and write *Sin* in between. To understand God's temporary arrangement for sin, read Leviticus 16:15-16. Cover the word *Sin* with a sheet of red paper. Explain that the Old Testament sacrificial system covered sin but did not take it away. Ask someone to read Hebrews 9:23-26. Ask what Christ did with sin. Remove the red paper and erase the word *Sin.* Declare that because of Christ's sacrifice nothing blocks fellowship between God and Christians.

5. Ask why God demanded blood for forgiveness. Read Hebrews 9:22. Ask why children might require signing names in blood when they form a club. Agree that you mean business when you shed blood. Read Leviticus 17:11. Declare: *Sin is so serious that only the lifeblood of God's own Son was sufficient enough to wipe it away.*

6. Comment that we might not grasp the concept of blood sacrifice, but we certainly understand the concept of debt. Request learners consider their present debts. Ask what plan they have to erase their debts. Request someone read Colossians 2:13-14. Request participants describe God's plan to erase our sin debt.

7. Comment that Christ pays our sin debt in full regardless of how much or how badly we have sinned. Discuss the second activity of Day 4. Ask: *How might some view this as unfair? Is it good or bad news to you? Why?*

8. Ask what hinders our ability to accept God's complete forgiveness. In Day 2 Dr. Stanley said people may come up with alternate systems to find forgiveness. Discuss what some of those alternate systems may be and why none of them are adequate.

9. Encourage participants to seriously consider (if they haven't already done so) the introspective questions at the end of Days 2 and 5. State that Christ paid the penalty for our sin so we can enjoy forgiveness free of charge. Encourage every participant to fully accept God's gift of forgiveness. Encourage them to read and complete each day's activities for Week 3 of this study. Close in prayer.

[1] Harry Verploegh, compiler and editor, *A. W. Tozer: An Anthology* (Camp Hill, PA: Christian Publications, 1984), 71.

[2] *www.brillig.com/debt_clock/.*

Faith and Forgiveness

day One

The Time Game

One of the most difficult habits for me to break was playing what I call the time game. It went like this. I would sin. I would feel guilty. I would ask God to forgive me. Then, depending on the magnitude of the sin, I would allow a certain amount of time to pass before I would ask God for things again. Sometimes I would wait an hour. Sometimes I would wait until the next day. I realize now that this was my way of punishing myself. But on the conscious level, I did it out of respect for God. I mean, God is forgiving and all that, but I felt I needed to give Him a little time to cool off before I started right back in with Him; I could not go on as if nothing happened. I understood all about the theology of forgiveness, but what I knew in my head had not taken hold of my heart and my emotions and my actions.

Many people share this problem. They nod their heads in agreement as the preacher expounds on the unconditional love of God and His desire to restore fellowship with lost men and women. Then you ask them, "Do you think God has really forgiven you?"

How would you answer if asked that question?
❏ **I don't see how He could.**
❏ **I hope so.**
❏ **I guess we really won't know until the end.**
❏ **I know God has forgiven me.**

For many Christians, a seed of doubt remains that all their personal sins are really forgiven, that God is genuinely not holding anything against them.

> "Therefore let us draw near with confidence to the throne of grace, so that we may receive mercy and find grace to help in time of need" (Heb. 4:16).

Until we are sure, until we settle the issue of forgiveness once and for all, two things will always be true. First, we will never have much confidence when we petition our Heavenly Father. We will always feel that God is holding something against us. Second, we will put others on the same scale we put ourselves on.

**Read Colossians 3:13 in your Bible.
What is to be our model for forgiveness?**

_____

If you think Christ's forgiveness is conditional and begrudging, what will your forgiveness of others be like?

_____

Since we are always trying to do something to ensure our forgiveness, we will subconsciously pressure others to perform to gain our forgiveness. We will have a tendency to remind others of their failures and their need to make up for them in some way.

A believer who functions in a "payback" mode in relation to personal standing before God is like a man who wins a car and continues to walk everywhere he goes. People comment on how beautiful the car is, and he agrees. He keeps it clean, he reads the owner's manual several times until he is thoroughly familiar with every facet of the car. Yet it does not accomplish for him what it was intended to accomplish. And it is all his fault. The car is no less his. But practically speaking, he might as well not own it. So it is with the believer who does not accept the forgiveness of God.

God wants us to live with perfect assurance that we are completely forgiven. To facilitate this, He has provided directions for making sure His gift of forgiveness has been applied to each individual's situation. In the last lesson we looked at the mechanics of forgiveness, how it all fits together. In this lesson we will look closely at the door through which each individual must pass to become a partaker of God's forgiveness.

The Dotted Line

The Old Testament Levitical laws delineated how an individual became a beneficiary of God's offer for atonement.

> **Read Leviticus 1:1-4 in your Bible.**
> **How did a person receive atonement for sin under the Old Testament system? Check all that apply.**
> ❑ **Sacrificed either all his belongings or his family**
> ❑ **Sacrificed a male animal without defect**
> ❑ **Danced, wept, and cut himself**
> ❑ **Laid his hand on the head of the sacrificial animal**

A man had to bring a sacrifice that met certain standards and sacrifice it on the altar. Not only did the one making the sacrifice have to bring an animal, but he also had to place his hand on its head as it was sacrificed. Thus he identified with the dying animal and God's promise of atonement was appropriated to his account.

What is the New Testament equivalent to the placing of the hand on the head of the sacrifice? Just as the Old Testament saints had to have a way of appropriating God's promises concerning forgiveness, so must we.

The point of identification for New Testament Christians is *faith*. Perhaps a better word is *trust*. To make God's gift of forgiveness our own, we must exercise faith. We must trust God to apply His work through Christ to our account when we sign on the dotted line of the certificate of pardon.

Now we need to consider something. Do we realize that every time we play the time game, or whatever games we play with God, we are turning our backs on God's means of ensuring our forgiveness and creating our own? What is worse, we are abandoning a system of faith for a system of works.

When we punish ourselves, whether it is by depriving ourselves of something or doing more than what is expected in some area, we treat God as if He requires some penance for our sin. We act as if a

Appropriate —to take for one's own use (Webster's New World Collegiate Dictionary).

112

demonstration of our sorrow earns forgiveness for us. We may feel better about ourselves when we demonstrate our sorrow in some way, but self-punishment has nothing to do with God's willingness to forgive. It has nothing to do with forgiveness at all. Yet every time we consciously or subconsciously work out some trade-off with God in regard to sin, we are abandoning His way for our way.

If we have placed our trust in God's system of forgiveness, we live in a forgiven state. From God's perspective, that means there is no difference between the sins we have committed, are committing, and will commit. None! Remember, forgiven is forgiven. In one sense, living in a state of forgiveness can be compared to having a checking account with unlimited funds available. In that financial condition we do not have to ask someone else to pay our debts for us. It would be impossible for us to incur debts as long as we write checks and continue to draw on our account.

This is exactly Paul's point when he writes, "And the Law came in that the transgression might increase, but where sin increased, grace abounded all the more, that, as sin reigned in death, even so grace might reign through righteousness to eternal life through Jesus Christ our Lord" (Rom. 5:20–21).

> **Write the correct mathematical symbol [= + < >] on the blank that best illustrates God's formula of forgiveness. God's Grace _____ My Sin**

There is always more grace than there is sin. Regardless of what is done or how many times it is done, it is already covered by God's grace. That is His willingness to consider it paid for in view of Christ's death. To work out our own system of merit is to say that God's grace is not sufficient for our sin, that He needs our help in dealing with our sin.

Our natural tendency is toward a work ethic in terms of our forgiveness. We find it difficult not to do *something* on our behalf. We are quick to give lip service to concepts such as *forgiveness comes through faith* and *we can do nothing to merit forgiveness*, but when it comes down to everyday living, we revert to a works-plus-faith system. That being the case, we need to understand the nature of faith and how it functions as the door into the realm of forgiveness. When we have made this idea our own, our behavior will be transformed. Our relationships with God and with others will be in accordance with what God intends for us, not what we intend for ourselves.

"We act as if a demonstration of our sorrow earns forgiveness for us. We may feel better about ourselves when we demonstrate our sorrow in some way, but self-punishment has nothing to do with God's willingness to forgive. It has nothing to do with forgiveness at all."—Charles Stanley

"To work out our own system of merit is to say that God's grace is not sufficient for our sin, that He needs our help in dealing with our sin."—Charles Stanley

Are there sins in your life that continue to make you feel guilty and miserable? Write those sins in the blanks below to complete your statement of faith. Read it out loud until you believe it.

God's grace is greater than _____

_____ .

day Three

"I Believe! I Think?"

Read Hebrews 11:6 in your Bible. Why is it absolutely essential to demonstrate faith in God's forgiveness in every area of your life?

_____

What is faith? What does it involve? These may seem to be somewhat elementary questions, but Christians answer in various ways and rarely do they respond with answers that fit the biblical data. A whole host of people seem to be confused about whether or not they have *really* believed. On the other hand, some people are certain they believe, but when pressed for details, they are not exactly sure *what* they believe; the content of their faith is undefined. Confusion or a lack of assurance in this area logically leads to confusion and doubts about forgiveness as well.

The use of the term *believe* in connection with forgiveness is not parallel to our common uses of the term. For instance, someone might say, "I believe it will snow tonight." In that case the term *believe* carries with it the idea of "calculated hope." That is, there is no guarantee it will snow; it is just a personal impression. Or a person might say, "I believe in God." In this case *believe* denotes mental assent to an idea. There is no sense of trust or commitment, just an acceptance of facts.

If we take these two unbiblical uses of the term *believe* and apply them to a discussion of forgiveness, we can understand how an individual can express belief in something and yet have no personal assurance. A person can say, "I believe God forgave me of my sin," and then turn right around and say, "I hope I am forgiven." There really is no contradiction for the person who uses the term to refer to a calculated hope.

> **Read Hebrews 11:1 in the margin. Complete the statements below to apply this definition of faith to forgiveness.**
>
> **I don't just hope I am forgiven; I am** _____.
>
> **I don't just believe I am forgiven; I am** _____.

"Now faith is the assurance of things hoped for, the conviction of things not seen" (Heb. 11:1).

In the same way, an individual who understands faith as mental assent to facts can say, "I believe God offers forgiveness through Christ" and yet have never had God's forgiveness applied to personal sin. Think about that. A man or a woman can verbally express faith and not be forgiven. The problem in both these examples is that neither person has expressed biblical faith.

> **Read Mark 9:24 in your Bible. If you are not utterly assured and convinced you are fully forgiven, make this father's prayer your own prayer as well.**

day Four

Biblical Faith

In discussing the meaning of biblical faith, the term *trust* should be substituted whenever *faith* or *believe* is being used in connection with forgiveness or salvation in general. *Webster's Third New International Dictionary* defines *trust* as: "assured reliance on some person or thing; a confident dependence on the character, ability, strength, or truth of someone or something."

The concept of trust denotes personal involvement. It assumes a relationship of some sort between the one expressing trust and the person or thing being trusted. The difference between belief and trust is the difference between acknowledging that the bridge is capable of holding a person's weight and actually walking out on the bridge. The former is simply the acknowledgment of something, with no involvement on the part of the one expressing faith; the latter is actual dependence.

Biblical faith, the type of faith that serves as the door to forgiveness, assumes a relationship of actual dependence and reliance. To state it using *Webster's* terms, biblical faith, or trust, is "the assured reliance on God: a confident dependence on the character, ability, strength, and truth of God and His promises."

The biblical support for this understanding of the term *believe* comes from a grammatical construct that occurs repeatedly when faith is spoken of in connection with forgiveness and salvation. This construct consists of the Greek word that means "believe" followed by a little word that is translated "in" or "on," depending on the context of the passage and the Bible version used.

I emphasize the use of these two words together because the expression was original with the New Testament writers. They used it 45 times. Yet there is no parallel to this construction in either the Greek version of the Old Testament or in the secular Greek literature of that day.

This means that the New Testament writers had to develop terminology as original as their message.

> **Read the following verses in your Bible and fill in the blanks to complete the verses.**
>
> **John 1:12: "But as many as received Him, to them He gave the right to become children of God, even to those who _____ _____ His name."**
>
> **John 2:23: "Now when He was in Jerusalem at the Passover, during the feast, many _____ _____ His name."**

The object of biblical faith, as regards forgiveness, is always the person or words of Jesus. By "object" I mean what people are being asked to put their faith in. For example, in the statement "Trust the car to get you there," the car is the object of faith. This is an important point because many people have faith, but it is directed in all sorts of inappropriate directions—or no direction at all.

The object of forgiving faith must be Christ, not simply God, the goodness of God, or faith itself.

Read John 14:1,6 in your Bible and complete the following statement.

Jesus said we are to believe in _____ and also in _____ because _____.

Jesus parallels *believing in Him* with *believing in God*. Then He turns right around and says that "no one" gets to God except through Him.

I mention this because many people have faith *in God* yet have never expressed faith *in Christ*. I meet men especially who express faith in God, but they leave Christ out of the picture altogether. They have faith, but the object of their faith is wrong or, perhaps I should say, limited.

Many people have faith in another god. They often respond by saying something to the effect that, "All religions lead to God; you choose your way, and I'll choose mine." This sounds so just and fair. And once again there is a genuine expression of faith. But it is faith man's way, not God's. It is real faith without a real foundation. It is sincere but uninformed faith. Forgiveness is available only to the man or woman who has put personal trust in Christ. For faith to accomplish its intended purpose, it must be focused in the right direction.

The New Testament writers were calling people to place their trust in the person of Jesus Christ for the forgiveness of their sins and the promise of eternal life. They were asking people to rely on or depend on Christ as the way to God and thus the way to forgiveness of sin. It was more than acknowledging that Christ was from God. It was more than hoping that what He said was true. It was a personal commitment to dependency upon Him for forgiveness. It was a matter of casting hopes for eternity upon the claims and promises of Jesus Christ. Such faith was (and still is) the way to forgiveness.

Read Romans 10:11 in your Bible. What promise do you have if you choose to put your faith in Jesus?

_____

_____

If you desire to dig deeper...

Read the following passages and note what comes to those who believe in Christ.
- John 3:14-18
- John 6:35-40
- John 7:38-39
- John 11:25
- Acts 10:43
- Acts 16:31-34

Appropriating the Gift

God's gift of forgiveness must be appropriated; that is, it must be accepted on an individual basis. Although it is a universal offer, it has no effect on the sin debt of a man or a woman who has not personally put trust in Christ. It is like a paycheck that is never picked up; it is like a gift certificate that is not redeemed; it is like a lifeline that is ignored by a drowning person.

Christ creatively communicated the concept of appropriation. Through the use of word pictures and parables, He used every conceivable illustration to show His audience that they needed to personally and individually appropriate God's gift of eternal life for themselves.

Christ constantly reiterated the need to appropriate His offer because the Jewish mind-set was such that the Jews believed they were automatically included in God's plan simply because of their nationality. Their confusion was similar to the confusion I find in many people today. Most people want to avoid the subject of accountability to God. Hearing the gospel may be bearable, but making a decision to place their trust in Christ to be the payment for their sin is going a step too far. They would much rather go on thinking about God as some benevolent force in the sky who loves everybody and who would not dare send anybody to hell. What they overlook is their responsibility to appropriate through faith God's gift of forgiveness.

> **Read Romans 10:9-10 in your Bible.**
> **What actions must you take before God declares you**
> **not guilty?** _____

WHAT ABOUT YOU?

That brings us to some important questions. Has there been a time in your life when you personally placed your trust in the death of Christ to be the payment for your sin? Have you appropriated His payment for your debt? Have you tasted the living water? Have you walked through the door that leads to salvation? Have you received eternal life?

If you answered no to any of these questions, turn to the inside front cover of this publication to discover how you can personally accept God's gift of forgiveness and eternal life.

Remember, *knowing* the truth is not enough. Understanding what Christ did is only the first step. Forgiveness comes through *trusting* in Christ. Regardless of what you have done or how many times you have done it or who you hurt in the process, complete forgiveness is available if you are willing to receive it. But it is available only through the death of Christ.

If, on the other hand, you know that you have placed your trust in the death of Christ for the payment of your sin, I can say to you with full assurance, "You are forgiven!"—past, present, and future. No more saying, "I hope so" or "I think so." You can say, "I know so!"

MEMORIALS AND REMINDERS

You may be thinking: *That's easy for you to say, but I am plagued by memories of the past. Every time I pray I think about the things I've done, and I feel alienated from God. I cannot pray with any confidence or assurance.*

If that is your situation, let me offer a practical exercise that will turn things around for you. First, you must settle in your mind once and for all that your sins are forgiven; that God is in no way holding them against you; that from His perspective, they are no longer obstacles to fellowship. That takes care of the mind aspect; now for the emotions.

Second, you must begin to view your past failures as reminders of God's grace. Your past sins should become memorials to the grace of God in your life. When Satan accuses you of being unworthy because of things you have done in the past, you can respond by saying (and I recommend actually speaking out loud), "That is exactly right. I did do that, and that's not all. But before I ever committed my first sin Jesus Christ died and paid for my sins—not just the ones you have reminded me of—all of them. Now they stand in my past as memorials, reminders of God's goodness and grace toward me. Thanks for the reminder."

This may seem like just a mental exercise, but more important, it is also a confession of truth. It confesses the truth you need to combat the lies of Satan. In time you will be able to rejoice at the thought of your past in connection with the grace of God as it was demonstrated at Calvary. Soon what once destroyed your assurance will become your greatest source of assurance.

> **How has the memory of a past sin actually become your greatest source of assurance in God's power and desire to forgive?**
>
> _____
>
> _____
>
> **If you are plagued by memories of past sins, how can that failure become your greatest source of assurance?**
>
> _____
>
> _____

To the Leader:

Meditate on Romans 4:1-8 this week. Have you been relying on faith or works to obtain forgiveness? Let this be the week you decide to finally and totally trust Christ to forgive all your sins. Then you can declare to your class with all conviction, "How happy the man [or woman] whom the Lord will never charge with sin!" (Rom. 4:8, HCSB).

Before the Session

1. Divide a poster board into four quadrants. Write "More Guilt" on one quadrant and cover with a sheet of paper you label "Door #1: Guilt." On the second quadrant write "Temporary Good Feelings" and cover with a sheet of paper labeled "Door #2: Good Works." Write "Frustration" on the third and cover with paper labeled "Door #3: Self-Punishment." On the fourth quadrant write "Forgiveness" and cover with paper labeled "Door #4: Faith." (For optional Step 1.)

2. Provide copies of the 1991 edition of the *The Baptist Hymnal*.

During the Session

1. Ask: *What have you discovered pleases your: spouse, children, pet, boss, parents? How do people attempt to please God? What is the only way we can please God?* Read Hebrews 11:6. Declare we please God when we place our faith in Him because that faith opens the door for Him to give us forgiveness.

OR

Invite participants to play "Let's Make a Deal with God." Display the poster you prepared earlier. Tell participants there is a fantastic gift behind one of those doors. Ask: *If people attempt to make a deal with God by feeling overly guilty for their sins, what will they receive?* After discussion, open "Door #1." Repeat this process with Doors #2 and #3, asking what people will receive if they attempt to make a deal with God by good works or self-punishment. Ask learners which door they would choose if they wanted total forgiveness. Open Door #4. Declare: *To receive forgiveness we don't make a deal with God; we simply walk through the door He has provided. Today we will discover how to open that door of faith.*

2. Read Jeremiah 31:34 and ask if participants think most Christians really believe that. Request they give a reason for their answers. Ask what games people play in an attempt to earn complete forgiveness. Request participants state the two reasons Dr. Stanley said Christians must settle the issue of whether or not God has fully forgiven them.

Discuss the last activity of Day 1 and explore why our forgiveness of others depends on our perception of God's forgiveness of us. Explain that is why this study on forgiving others has so far focused on understanding God's forgiveness. You can't fully forgive others if you don't believe you are fully forgiven.

3. Explain Dr. Stanley's illustration from Day 2 of forgiveness being like an unlimited checking account. Invite someone to read Romans 5:20-21. Distribute the hymnals. Direct participants to read silently the words to Hymn 329, *Grace Greater Than Our Sin.* Ask learners to state how the hymn writer described God's grace. Inquire: *What does God's grace do? What must we do to receive this marvelous grace?* Declare that the hymn writer said all that is necessary is to believe and receive. So it's imperative to understand what it means to believe.

4. Ask how someone can express belief in God or His ability to forgive yet still not be assured he or she is completely forgiven. [He or she is speaking of belief in terms of hope or mental assent.] Discuss the second activity in Day 3. Explain that complete assurance and conviction of faith can also be defined as trust. Ask someone to read the definition of trust from Day 4. Ask learners if they believe in airplanes. Inquire: *How do you demonstrate that you trust airplanes?* Agree that trusting requires personal involvement to get on that plane. Request participants read the completed verses from the first activity of Day 4. Note that the New Testament phrase "believe in" means that one completely entrusts his or her life to Christ. Ask volunteers to read the Scriptures in the "Dig Deeper" activity in the margin of Day 4. Ask what we can completely trust Christ to do for us.

5. Read John 4:39-42. Ask what important principle about belief the Samaritan townspeople demonstrated. [Each individual must choose to believe in Christ for him or herself.] Ask how each individual person can demonstrate he or she has chosen to trust Christ for forgiveness. [See the first activity of Day 5 to help answer that question.] Urge any participant who would like to place his or her faith in Christ to speak with you or to your pastor.

6. Read Romans 10:11. Assure participants Christ will never disappoint them if they put their faith in Him. Discuss the final activity of Day 5 in the margin on page 119.

7. Close in prayer.

Our Forgiving Father

day One

A Worst-Case Scenario

How do you picture God when you think about your sin? What do you think His expression is when you come to Him with the same old sin time and time again? What do you think His attitude is toward you in light of your failures? Like most Christians, you would probably acknowledge that God loves you. But do you think He *likes* you?

For many people, these are especially difficult questions. The term *Father* does not bring with it feelings of love and acceptance. Instead it conjures up feelings of fear, dread, hurt, and disappointment. These feelings associated with an earthly father have the potential of robbing us of the assurance of forgiveness the Heavenly Father sacrificed so deeply for us to experience.

We are not the first generation to struggle with a distorted view of God's attitude toward sinners. To correct this thinking, Jesus told a series of parables in Luke 15.

> **Read Luke 15:1-3 in your Bible. Why do you think Jesus told these parables?**
> ❑ **To defend Himself against the Pharisee's criticism**
> ❑ **To assure the Pharisees they were still God's favorites**
> ❑ **To assure the "sinners" they were fine just the way they were**
> ❑ **To explain God's true attitude toward sinners**

The last in the series of parables is the one we know as the parable of the prodigal son. By looking at this insightful parable, we can pick up on God's attitude toward sinners and His motivation for sending Christ to die. It is my prayer that through this lesson God will begin to deal with you on an emotional level so that whatever is keeping you from experiencing the joy and peace of knowing you are forgiven will be put to rest. Whether you are a victim of incorrect teaching or you were mistreated by your earthly father—whatever the stumbling block may be—God wants to take it out of the way and flood you with the assurance of His forgiveness and acceptance. He wants you to live with a sense of security and intimacy with Him.

Take some time to refamiliarize yourself with the parable in Luke 15:11-23. Jesus gives us this parable of the lost son to help us understand God the Father's attitude toward us when we sin against Him. Since He illustrates His point by reference to a father-son relationship where the son has sinned against the father, it should be obvious that the message is for those who are already of the household of faith, that is, believers. It is particularly aimed at those persons living under the awesome load of uncertainty of knowing they have displeased God.

When we understand the culture of the day, we see that Jesus could not have pictured the prodigal in a more degrading manner.

List all the ways you can find in Luke 15:11-16 that the son conducted himself in a degrading manner.

_____

_____

Did you spot all the items mentioned in the margin?

Why did Jesus picture the prodigal in such an extreme fashion? He was trying to help us understand something basic about forgiveness. The young man's sinfulness was such that there was nothing left in him that could motivate his father to forgive him. His father forgave him because it was his nature to love and thus to forgive.

Like the father in the parable, God forgives because it is His nature to forgive. Nothing we can do on our own can prompt God to forgive us. It is His character that moves Him, not ours.

"First of all, in his selfish egotism he asked for his share of the inheritance. The custom was for the father to give the inheritance at the time he chose. It would have been unheard of for a son, especially a younger son, to ask for his inheritance. Jesus' audience would have viewed his actions as a sign of great disrespect, maybe even as grounds for disinheritance. Second, he took it all and left. The custom would have been for him to stick around and care for his aging parents. Sons were to make sure that their fathers were buried properly and that their mothers were provided for. This son took off with no regard for his family. Third, he spent his entire inheritance in a relatively short time. His father had taken a lifetime to accumulate it, and it represented years of hard work and wise stewardship. Yet the younger son spent it all on short-lived pleasure. Fourth, after he had run out of money and the famine hit, he did the most despicable thing a Jewish man could do—he took a job caring for hogs. Not cows or sheep, but pigs."—Charles Stanley

day Two

A Surprising Response

When Jesus got to the part of the story where He described the son's desire to return home, I can only imagine the Pharisees' feelings as they thought about what they would do if they had a son who behaved in such a manner. No doubt they were shocked at how Jesus closed the story. Read about the son's return in the margin.

HOW FAR IS TOO FAR?

This "surprise ending" reveals several marvelous facets of God's attitude toward returning sinners. First, *our Heavenly Father's love has no limits.* If there had been a limit on how far the father was willing to stretch before cutting his son off completely, certainly the young man had gone too far. He did everything wrong.

The point is clear. A man or a woman cannot go so far that God's love and forgiveness are no longer offered. The father would have accepted the son back at any time. The son was forgiven before he ever returned.

> **Read 2 Peter 3:9 in your Bible. What is the reason for God's patience with you?**

_____

Regardless of what you have done, you have not stretched God beyond His limits. His love knows no limits. Your sin was dealt with two thousand years ago when Christ died. As far as He is concerned, you live in a state of forgiveness.

HOW LONG IS TOO LONG?

We do not know how long the son had been gone. It was long enough for him to spend a great deal of money, suffer through a famine, and hold down a job. Jesus did not give us a time frame. It was really irrelevant to His point. And yet it was part of the point. *Our Heavenly Father's love is*

"The son finally realized the futility of his ways and decided to go home. There was no mention of his cleaning himself up. As far as we know, he did not even attempt to make himself presentable to his father. He just headed home in the most despicable condition possible.

"When the father saw his son coming down the road, he ran toward him, hugged him, and kissed him. He showered his affection upon the dirty, bedraggled, hog-feeding son of his who had squandered his inheritance and embarrassed the family. He seemed unconcerned about where his son had been or what he had done; his focus was on his son who had returned."
—Charles Stanley

patient. The story seems to indicate that the boy's father made it a habit of looking in the direction the boy had gone, hoping to see him returning. He was willing to restore his son no matter when he returned.

In the same way, your Heavenly Father waits patiently for you when you leave for a season of sin. He does not sit and scheme about the things He will do to you once you return. Because He desires to have unbroken fellowship with you, He wants you to return. He wants you to take advantage of the depth of relationship He has made possible for you through Christ.

PATIENT BUT EAGER

Third, *God is also eager to express His love.*

Read Luke 15:20 in your Bible. How did the father display his eagerness to welcome his son?

_____

In New Testament times no one who had any dignity ran in public. But when the father saw the son coming down the road, he ran. This detail must have stunned the scribes and Pharisees. That was not the way they imagined God at all. They saw Him as a God who delighted in chastising sinners.

Do you realize that God is more eager to reestablish fellowship after you sin than you are? You can be assured of that by looking at what He did to make fellowship with Him possible to begin with. He can't wait for you to turn back to Him.

God is not sitting on His throne with a black notebook in one hand and a whip in the other waiting for you to return so that He can read off all you have done and chastise you for it. Like the father in the parable, He is eagerly waiting for you to return so He can restore you and clean you up.

THE FOCUS OF THE FATHER

A fourth facet of God the Father's attitude is that *His focus is on the sinner,* not the sin. Upon returning, the son immediately began to recite his prepared speech in verse 21. His focus, like ours, was on his sin, his unworthiness. In essence he was begging for mercy. He readily acknowledged his father's right to reject his request for charity. He knew what he deserved, and he was willing to take what was coming.

> **Read Luke 15:21-23.**
> **What was the father's focus? (Circle one.)**
>
> **The sin**   **The son**

"But what about the son's sin? What about all the money he wasted? What about the embarrassment he caused the family?" we may ask. Those were not the father's concerns. He had one thing, and one thing only, on his mind: "For this son of mine was dead, and has come to life again; he was lost, and has been found" (Luke 15:24).

God has dealt with your sin. It is no longer His focus. *You* are His focus. To God, your sin is no longer a hindrance to His fellowship with you. It is a hindrance only as long as you allow the guilt that accompanies sin to blind you to the fact that God is eager to reestablish fellowship with you.

Once you turn back to God, He is eager to take you back immediately. What you have done or how long you have done it is never a consideration. The father in the parable did not know what had happened to his son, where he had been, or how he had lost his money. And he did not ask. His son was back, and that was the only thing that mattered.

A JOYFUL WELCOME

We need to consider a fifth and final facet of God's attitude toward returning sinners. This one gives us great insight into the heart of God. *God receives the sinner back into fellowship joyfully.*

We see this in two statements Jesus made. First, He said, "But while he was still a long way off, his father saw him, and felt compassion for him" (Luke 15:20). Think about this. Jesus portrayed the Heavenly Father in such a way that His immediate response to a returning sinner was compassion. Not anger, not frustration, not indignation—all of which we might think He would have been justified in feeling—but compassion.

When we are confronted with people who have hurt us or abused our relationship with them, our initial response—the one that just happens without our planning it—is usually anger or hurt. Then if we are really "spiritual," we may try to deal with those emotions by asking God to help us see things from His perspective. In time we can usually relate to those individuals in a civilized manner without blowing up and telling them how we feel.

That is what makes the father's first emotional response even more amazing to us. Out of his compassion he identified with the hurt and misery of his son, and he wanted to alleviate that pain. His own hurt did not get in the way of his ability to identify with his son's hurt.

So it is with the Heavenly Father when you return to Him from your sin. He has dealt with the personal hurt your sin caused Him. His focus is not on that. Alleviating your pain and sorrow results in joy on His behalf.

We also see this idea of joy in Jesus' statement: "And they began to be merry" (Luke 15:24). It was a time of celebration for the father, and he threw a big party. His greatest desire had been fulfilled; his son had come home.

When you or any child of God turns from sin, God rejoices. He "feels" compassion for you and experiences joy at your homecoming. He does not wrestle with feelings of hurt and jealously. He has dealt with that once and for all. Instead, He identifies with your hurt and frustration and takes joy in seeing you set free.

> **Read Isaiah 30:18-19 in your Bible (in several transla-tions if possible).**
> **Record phrases that convey to you:**
>   **1. the limitless nature of God's love**
>   **2. the patience of God's love**
>   **3. God's eagerness to express His love**
>   **4. God's focus on His child**
>   **5. God's joyful welcome**

ACCEPT GOD'S TRUE CHARACTER

I imagine it was difficult for many of those listening to Jesus to change their thinking about God and His attitude toward sinners. What about you? Are you willing to accept what Christ said about your Heavenly Father? You have a forgiving Father whose love and patience are unlimited. You cannot push Him too far. He is eager to have fellowship with you. You have a Heavenly Father who is free to identify with your situation and who takes great joy in seeing you restored to your rightful place as His child. Your forgiving Father's greatest concern is you, not your sin. His focus is on you and your willingness to comply with His will for your life. Begin now renewing your mind by thinking about these five tremendous facts about the character of God. A good way to start would be to pray the simple prayer in the margin that incorporates all that we have seen about the character of God in this lesson.

"Heavenly Father, sometimes it is difficult for me to see You as You really are. By faith in the testimony of Jesus, however, I accept you as my forgiving Heavenly Father. A Father who loves me with unlimited love. A Father whose patience is inexhaustible. A Father who is eager to have fellowship with me. A Father who focuses on me and my position as Your child, not on my sin. A Father who rejoices when I turn to You from my sin whether it be one single act or a season of rebellion. Expose the errors in my thinking toward You and fill me with the truth, for I know that in discovering the truth I will be set free. Amen."
—Charles Stanley

Forgiveness and Confession

Now that we have examined God's part in forgiveness, what about our responsibility? You may be asking at this point, "Do we even have a responsibility? It sounds as if God has taken care of the whole thing from beginning to end."

Remember, however, that the parable of the prodigal son portrays not only a forgiving father but also a returning son. What about him?

> **Read Luke 15:17-19 and complete the "I" statements the son made.**
>
> I am_____.
>
> I will go _____.
>
> I will say _____.
>
> I will acknowledge _____.

Out of a spirit of futility, hopelessness, and humility the son made a decision to return to his father. He rehearsed what he would say and upon falling into his father's arms he confessed, "I have sinned against heaven and in your sight; I am no longer worthy to be called your son."

CONFESSION AND FORGIVENESS

It is vital to note that before the prodigal could confess his failure to his father, "his father saw him, and felt compassion for him, and ran and embraced him, and kissed him." The son's acceptance and forgiveness were not conditional upon his confession. The father was not motivated to forgive based on his son's confession of a life of sin. He fell into the arms of a father whose forgiveness was constant from the moment he walked away.

Then why does the Bible teach that we are to confess our sins if we are already forgiven? What is the role of confession? If we are already forgiven, it seems unnecessary, doesn't it? What is the place of confession in God's strategy for our forgiveness?

The Greek word we use for *confess* means "to agree with." When we confess our sins to our Heavenly Father, we are agreeing with Him. We are agreeing with His attitude about sin; that is, sin is against Him, it is destructive to His purpose for our lives, and it carries with it consequences that will prove painful. Confession also implies that we are assuming responsibility for our actions. We are not blaming our actions on others. Confession means that we see ourselves in relationship to our deeds of sin just as God does.

FIRST JOHN 1:9

Undoubtedly the most often quoted verse regarding confession is 1 John 1:9: "If we confess our sins, He is faithful and righteous to forgive us our sins and to cleanse us from all unrighteousness." When taken at face value, the verse would seem to indicate that our forgiveness is conditional upon our confession. This raises all kinds of questions: What if we forget to confess a sin? What if we don't realize we have committed a sin? And on and on we could go.

All of a sudden we have lost sight of what Christ has done on the cross, and we are focusing our attention on our memory and our sensitivity to sin. But the basis of our forgiveness is not confession, repentance, or faith, though all three are essential to our experience of forgiveness. The basis of our forgiveness is the sacrificial, substitutionary death of Jesus Christ on the cross. His death as the sinless Son of God paid in full the penalty for all our sins—past, present, and future. We can add nothing to Christ's death that will gain for us any more forgiveness than we already have. That forgiveness becomes a reality in the life of every person who by faith receives Christ as Savior. And after we are saved, the basis of our continuing forgiveness is still none other than the shed blood of Christ at Calvary.

Read 1 John 2:1-2 in your Bible. When you sin:

What action has Jesus already taken on your behalf?

_____

What further action will He take on your behalf?

_____

A Family Affair

The confusion over confession hinges on our tendency to assign certain definitions to words without regard to the context in which they are used. When we come to the concept of forgiveness, we must be careful not to assume that a biblical author is always talking about the forgiveness a believer experiences when he or she first puts trust in Christ. Forgiveness in that sense is the door leading to a relationship with God. That type of forgiveness is a one-time-only phenomenon. Once pardoned, always pardoned.

The individual who becomes a child of God, thus establishing an eternal relationship with the Heavenly Father, begins to relate to God in a new way. The new believer has new rights as well as new responsibilities. After the individual has become a partaker of eternal life, a new set of guidelines governs the relationship with God. One of these new guidelines has to do with restoring fellowship with the Heavenly Father after the believer sins. The believer must receive what someone has termed "familial forgiveness."

Eternal salvation and forgiveness of the debt of sin separating us from God are not the issues here. This is a matter of family business. So John includes himself when he writes, "If *we* confess *our* sins." Until we turn back to God from our sin, fellowship is broken. When we as believers come to God confessing our sins, the confession does not persuade God to forgive us. He did that at the cross. The confession restores us to our previous level of fellowship and intimacy with Him. Confession is essential, not to receive forgiveness but to experience the forgiveness God has provided through the death of Christ and to have unhindered fellowship with Him.

But there is more. In confession we experience release from guilt, tension, pressure, and emotional stress resulting from our sins. Failure to confess our sins ensures the continuation of those unnecessary negative feelings.

Read Psalm 32:1-5 in your Bible.
Describe the psalmist's physical and mental condition before he confessed his sin.

_____

How did the psalmist feel after his confession (vv. 1-2)?

_____

Failure to understand the purpose and place of confession can result in fear and uncertainty about our salvation; it takes the cutting edge off our joy; it leaves us with a nagging doubt that deprives us of the peace our Lord intends for His children. If we are not clear about the nature and power of our confession, our service for God will be hindered. Our ambivalence will short-circuit our motivation to serve God because we will not feel worthy or competent. We will have a nagging sense of guilt: *I wonder what God thinks of me? I wonder if He is pleased with me?* The cloud of doubt will continually hang over us: *Have I confessed everything? Am I sorry enough for my sins?* When we understand our true position in Christ, these thoughts will no longer harass us. We will be able to confess our sins and, on the basis of Christ's shed blood, accept our forgiveness and thank God for His great grace toward us.

Describe a time you personally experienced the truth that "Confession is good for the soul."

_____

leader Guide

To the Leader:

Do you honestly feel like God likes you? Read Zephaniah 3:16-17 out loud several times. (Zephaniah really is in the Bible! Use the Table of Contents.) God really does like you! He delights in you even more than you delight in your child or grandbaby! You bring Him so much joy He just has to sing! Spend some time this week expressing and receiving mutual delight with your forgiving Father.

During the Session

1. Ask: *Can you recall a time growing up when you realized someone did not like you? How did it affect the way you felt and acted? How did you feel and behave when you discovered someone liked you? How do you think it would change people's lives if they realized God likes them?*

OR

Request participants demonstrate expressions of disgust, exasperation, disappointment, and compassion. Ask which expression many people think God wears when His children approach Him with their sin.

2. Ask why many people have a distorted view of God. Comment that a sincere look at God's Word can change those distorted perceptions. Ask someone to read Luke 15:1-3. Ask: *What was the religious leaders' accusation against Jesus? How did this reflect their distorted view of God?* Discuss the first activity of Day 1. Invite someone to read Luke 15:4-10. Ask questions such as: *What lessons about God did Jesus teach in these two parables? How was He responding to the Pharisee's accusations? Do you think the Pharisees got it? Why?*

3. Explain that the first two parables emphasize how God seeks sinners and rejoices when they are found. The parable of the prodigal son describes how a child moves away from his father and how the father joyfully welcomes him back. Request someone read Luke 15:11-16. Inquire: *Why do you think the younger son wanted to leave home? Was he ready? Should the father have given him what he demanded? Why or why not?* Discuss the second activity in Day 1. Ask why Jesus described this young man in the worst possible light.

4. Read Luke 15:17-20a (stop at "he got up and went to his father"). Ask: *What do you think the Pharisees were thinking about the boy at this point? How do you think they expected the father to respond?* Request someone read Luke 15:20b-24. Lead a discussion with questions such as: *Why do you think the father saw him when he was still a long way off? Do you think God waits and watches for you to return? What expression do you think God wears as He waits? How do*

you think the son expected the father to respond when he returned? How do you think he felt and acted at the father's amazing reception?

5. Ask: *What's your limit on putting up with people? What's God's limit?* Read Psalm 103:8-12. Discuss how this first facet of God's attitude toward returning sinners answers people's excuse that they've sinned too badly for God to ever love them. Ask participants to name the second facet of God's attitude toward sinners and discuss that activity. Ask: *How often, aside from exercise, do you run? Why?* Discuss the last activity in Day 2. Ask how that demonstrated the magnitude of the father's love for his son. Ask: *What does this say to you about God's love for you?*

6. Ask if participants recall reading *The Scarlet Letter* in school. Ask what letter Hester Prynne had to wear and why. [A scarlet "A" on her chest to publicize that she was an adulteress.] Ask: *Do you ever feel like all God sees when He looks at you is a big "S" for sinner or "L" for loser? What does God really focus on when you return to Him? What is the only thing that matters to God when you return to Him?*

7. Invite volunteers to share how they felt when someone threw them a big party. Ask participants how they feel to know God throws a big party when they return to Him. Discuss how the five facets of God's attitude toward sinners revealed in this parable have helped change participants' perceptions of God.

8. Discuss the son's responsibility in this parable. Ask: *Did he have to return home to receive forgiveness or to experience the forgiveness the father already had for him? What's the difference?* Ask someone to read 1 John 1:9. Discuss Dr. Stanley's question, "Why does the Bible teach we are to confess our sins if we are already forgiven?" Request participants state negative consequences of not confessing sin. Use the first activity of Day 5 to add to the discussion. Guide participants to understand that forgiveness is not conditioned on confession but our joy and intimacy with God are. Invite volunteers to share their responses to the final activity.

Handling Our Hurts

day One

Developing an Unforgiving Spirit, Part 1

An unforgiving spirit does not develop overnight. It involves a process of responses and thus takes time to develop. In talking with people through the years I have discovered 10 stages an individual is likely to go through. Not everyone will pass through each stage, but almost everyone I have known with an unforgiving spirit could identify with several of them.

WE GET HURT

The seeds of an unforgiving spirit are planted when we are wronged or hurt in some way. It could be a physical, an emotional, or a verbal hurt. It could be a hurt we experienced in childhood or adulthood. It really makes no difference. Since we live in such a self-centered world, often we experience our first hurt as a child, and unfortunately, this early hurt usually comes from the people we love and respect the most.

> **Read Psalm 55:20-21 in your Bible. Who was hurting David?** ❑ **His political opponent** ❑ **His friend** ❑ **His long-time enemy**
> **How was this person hurting David?**_____

All our hurts are really some form of rejection. We may not perceive it as rejection initially, but that is what happens when we are wronged by others. We may feel hurt, pain, abandonment, embarrassment, hatred, or some other negative emotion. But it all relates to rejection.

Feeling rejected is the first stage in developing an unforgiving spirit. That being the case, we all have the potential for problems in this area. Therefore, we must always be on our guard to stop the process in its beginning stages.

WE BECOME CONFUSED

Often our initial response to hurt, regardless of the form it takes, is confusion. We experience a sense of bewilderment; we are not quite sure how to respond. It is similar to being in a state of shock. In this stage, we may think, *This is not really happening*. We may even have a physical reaction, such as a deep feeling of emptiness in the pit of the stomach. Many people have actually gotten sick after experiencing rejection. This stage is usually short-lived, and immediately we move into the third stage.

Read Psalm 55:12-14. What question might David have wanted to ask this disloyal friend?

_____

WE LOOK FOR DETOURS

We all have a desire to avoid pain. Because of that, when we are hurt emotionally, instead of thinking about it we need to find ways of avoiding those painful thoughts or memories. We take mental detours. We don't allow ourselves to think about certain things. We change the subject when certain topics are brought up. This desire to detour around past hurt motivates many people to drink heavily or to become addicted to both prescription and nonprescription drugs. The fact is, I have never counseled a drug addict or an alcoholic who was not trying to cover up the pain of the past. The root problem was never alcohol or drugs; it was always the inability to cope with rejection.

Read Psalm 55:6-8. What did David want to do about this painful situation?

_____

_____

WE DIG A HOLE

After we try to "schedule" around our hurt, that is, to arrange our thought patterns and lives in general so as never to come into contact with anything that reminds us of our hurt (an undertaking that is rarely successful), we attempt to forget the whole thing ever occurred. We dig a hole and bury it as deeply as we can.

WE DENY IT

The fifth stage is also one of denial. We deny that we were ever hurt or that we are covering up anything. We smile and say, "Oh, I have dealt with that." Or "I forgave him long ago."

This is a tough stage for people to break out of. I have met scores of adults who are carrying around a load of bitterness, as demonstrated through their tempers or other negative behavior, but they see no connection between a turbulent childhood and their problems as adults.

day Two

Developing an Unforgiving Spirit, Part 2

WE BECOME DEFEATED

Regardless of how successfully we think we have buried our hurt, it will still work its way out through our behavior. A short temper, oversensitivity, shyness, a critical spirit, jealously—all of these can be evidence of un-resolved rejection. The tragedy is that when we deny that we are harboring hurt, we will look everywhere but the right place for a way to change the resulting undesirable behavior. We can move, change jobs, change friends, rededicate our lives, make New Year's resolutions, memorize Scripture, pray long prayers, fast, or undertake any number of spiritual exercises. But until we deal with the root of the problem, we will ultimately be defeated in our attempts to change.

> **Circle the adjectives that describe you.**
> **Short tempered**   **Depressed**   **Hypersensitive**
> **Critical**   **Jealous**   **None of these**
>
> **Underline the actions in the paragraph above that you have taken to attempt to rid yourself of these behaviors. Have they worked?** ❑ Yes ❑ No ❑ Sort of
>
> **If no, are you willing to consider whether you have not resolved a pain of rejection in your life?**
> ❑ Yes   ❑ No   ❑ I'm not sure

WE BECOME DISCOURAGED

This is the critical stage. It is usually the stage where we either seek professional help or bail out of our present circumstances altogether. After a while it seems as if things will never change or never get any better. Any little bit of progress we may see is always shattered by another incident that just confirms the suspicion that it's hopeless!

This is the stage in which husbands leave their wives either because their wives will not change or because they are unable to rekindle that "loving feeling" they once had. This is the stage in which women begin to depend on alcohol and prescription drugs to make it through the day.

An unforgiving spirit destroys respect. If allowed to go unchecked, it can dissolve the loyalty and even the sense of duty that are so necessary to hold a marriage together during difficult times. Extramarital affairs become a viable option to people who have publicly spoken out against adultery. Divorce becomes a real option to couples who pledged an unconditional lifetime of commitment. For those who can foresee no better circumstances in this life, they often choose to escape by taking their own lives. Such is the power and the poison of an unforgiving spirit.

> **If you are on the verge of bailing out, will you right now commit to do whatever it takes to get rid of your unforgiving spirit so you can be free?**
> **If so, write a prayer of commitment in the margin.**

WE DISCOVER THE TRUTH

For some of us, there is a happy ending. Through someone's help or by God's grace, we discover the root of bitterness. We gain insight into why we act the way we do. We are able to see the connection between the past and the present. The pieces finally fit together.

WE TAKE RESPONSIBILITY

The ninth stage is closely associated with the eighth one. In this stage we own up to our responsibility. We decide to quit blaming others. We decide to quit waiting for everybody and everything else around us to change. We open our hearts for God to have His way, regardless of how it might hurt.

> **Read Psalm 55:16-17,22-23. How did David deal with his pain?**

WE ARE DELIVERED

The final outcome for those of us who are willing to deal with an unforgiving spirit is deliverance. My friend, you can be free of that embarrassing, inappropriate, family-splitting behavior. You say, "But you don't know what has happened to me. You don't know what I have been through." You are right. But I have known people in all kinds of circumstances who have been delivered and restored.

day Three

So What Are You Waiting For?

You may be using the excuse that your circumstances are so bad that you could never forgive the person or persons who hurt you. The fact is, however, that you can if you are willing to. If you are not willing to forgive, you will ultimately bring your own life crashing down around you. It will be nobody else's fault but your own.

If you are unwilling to forgive, you have one (or more) of several problems. First, your unwillingness could be a result of *selfishness*. You have been hurt. Something unfair has happened to you. You did not get your way. Your thoughts have turned inward, and you are concerned only with yourself, your rights, and your feelings. You are waiting for the world to come to you and ask forgiveness before you are willing to forgive. *After all*, you think, *it was that other person's fault*. You live in a prison made of your emotions and expectations. It is selfishness because you have the ability to do something about it if you choose. You just may be too selfish to make the first move.

Perhaps your problem is *pride*. When there is pride in a heart, it is very difficult to be forgiving. Pride steps into the forefront of your thinking and says, "Look what they have done to me. If I forgive them, people will think I am weak and I do not have any backbone."

Pride tells you to somehow get back at those who have hurt you. Harboring anger in your heart makes you feel as if you are getting revenge; in fact, it only destroys you. The real problem is that when you set out to get revenge—even if it is only in your mind—you are assuming a responsibility that has been given to Christ and Christ alone.

"Pride goes before destruction, and a haughty spirit before stumbling" (Prov. 16:18).

Read Romans 14:10-12 in your Bible. Consider an action by another that has hurt you.
Who is to be the judge in that situation? (Circle one.)

Judge Judy   You   God   Your mother

Whose actions are you responsible for in that painful situation?

_____

God is the Judge. At the right time those who have hurt you will pay the penalty for their sin. In the meantime, you are to forgive.

A third reason you may not be willing to forgive is that you are struggling with *low self-esteem*. People with low self-esteem feel insignificant to begin with. Often, without really understanding what is taking place, they will attach their significance to the wrong they suffered. They are constantly saying things like this: "You know I would not be here if it were not for . . . I could have gone far if I had not lost my job with . . ." The unfair circumstances become a point of reference for everything else in their lives.

When this happens to people, they cannot afford to forgive. To deal with the hurt they suffered would be to take away the thing most essential to their identity. They would no longer get the sympathy from others they have come to rely on. They would have no more sad stories to tell. They would have no more excuses for their lack of diligence and discipline.

Do you have a habit of always bringing up a particular event in your life when you were treated unfairly? Without knowing it, you may have allowed your identity to become intertwined with an event you need to put behind you. Your true and eternal identity is found in your relationship with God through Christ. To experience the joy and freedom available to you in Christ, you must forgive those who have wronged you and move on.

Another reason you may be unwilling to deal with your unforgiving spirit is that *you think you already have*. Sometime in your past you may have acknowledged that you were wronged. You may have admitted that you "needed" to forgive others. You may have even prayed a prayer in which you said the words "I forgive _____." You may have meant it with all your heart, yet if there is evidence emotionally and verbally that something is still gnawing at you on the inside, if you are still uncomfortable around the people who wronged you or if things that remind you of them still make you become tense on the inside, chances are you have not completely dealt with the situation.

A fifth reason a person refuses to forgive is that it is *painful*. Being willing to forgive is painful in the sense that thinking about past hurts often brings back the original unpleasant emotions. Forgiveness can be especially painful if the wrong hurt so deeply that the pain suffered was buried and forgotten. The very thought of digging that back up, which is sometimes necessary, causes many people to run.

If you live with events in your past that are painful to even think about, please accept by faith that it is worth the pain in order to be set free. God wants to perform spiritual surgery. He wants to remove the bitterness and the hurt. It will hurt, but it will heal. And whatever scar may be left will be much easier to live with than the open wound you now bear.

There is one last reason: *You don't know how to be forgiving.* Maybe you are at the point of being able to say, "I am ready. Just tell me what to do." I hope so.

> **Record the six reasons people may be unwilling to forgive. Check the reasons you've been holding on to an unforgiving spirit.**
> **1.** _____
> **2.** _____
> **3.** _____
> **4.** _____
> **5.** _____
> **6.** _____

day *Four*

The Five Steps In Forgiveness

Forgiveness is an act of the will that involves five steps.

WE ARE FORGIVEN

First, we must recognize that *we have been totally forgiven.* Most people get hung up on this point. Once we understand the depth of our sin and the distance it put between us and God and once we get a glimpse of the sacrifice God made to restore fellowship with us, we should not hesitate to get involved in the process of forgiveness. To understand what God did for us and then to refuse to forgive those who have wronged us is to be like the wicked, ungrateful slave Jesus described in Matthew 18:23–34. Read that passage in your Bible now.

We read the parable and think, *How could anyone be so ungrateful?* But the believer who will not forgive another is even more guilty and more ungrateful than that slave.

> ## Read Matthew 18:35. What was Jesus' purpose in telling that parable?

_____

The first step, then, is to realize that we have been totally forgiven of a debt we could never pay and thus have no grounds for refusing to forgive others.

FORGIVE THE DEBT

The second step is to *release the person from the debt* we think is owed us for the offense. This must be a mental, an emotional, and sometimes even a physical release. It involves mentally bundling up all our hostile feelings and surrendering them to Christ.

We can accomplish this in one of two ways: either by meeting face-to-face or by using a substitute. Both work equally well, but one may be more appropriate than the other. In cases where a person is dead, lives far away, or is totally unapproachable, it will be necessary to use the chair-substitute method (see explanation in the margin).

ACCEPT OTHERS

The third step is to *accept others as they are* and release them from any responsibility to meet our needs.

VIEW OTHERS AS TOOLS OF GROWTH

Fourth, we must *view those we have forgiven as tools in our lives* to aid us in our growth in and understanding of the grace of God.

Joseph certainly understood this principle. After all his brothers did to him, he was able to forgive them. He saw them as the instruments of God to get him to Egypt and to be in such a position of power that he could save his family when the famine destroyed all the crops. So when his brothers fell down before him, fearful of what he might do to them to get even, he was able to say those famous words in Genesis 50:19–21.

The Chair-Substitute Method

1. Take two chairs and arrange them facing each other. Seat yourself in one of the chairs.

2. Imagine that the person you need to forgive is sitting in the other chair. Disclose everything you can remember that the person has done to hurt you. Do not hold back the tears or the emotions that accompany the confessions.

3. *Choose by an act of your will to forgive that person once and for all time.* You may not feel like being forgiving. Just do it and the feelings will follow. God will take care of that. Do not doubt that what you have done is real and valid.

4. Release the person from the debt you feel is owed you for the offense. Say, *"You are free and forgiven."*

5. If the person is still a part of your life, now is a good time to accept the individual without wanting to change aspects of his or her personality or behavior.

6. Thank the Lord for using each person as a tool in your life to deepen your insight into His grace and to conform you to the image of His Son.

Read Genesis 50:19-21 in your Bible.
If you are ready to be free of bitterness against a person who has harmed you, write that person's name in the blank below. Then read the statement out loud and mean it!

_____, you intended to harm me but God intended it for good. I release you from your debt.

MAKE RECONCILIATION

The last thing we must do is to *make reconciliation* with those from whom we have been estranged. This will vary from situation to situation. But if there is a family member, distant relative, former employee, or maybe an ex-friend we have avoided because we had hostility in our hearts against that person, we need to reestablish contact. We may have to begin by apologizing. Regardless of how we go about it, we must do what we can to restore fellowship with those who hurt us. Once our forgiveness is complete, reconciliation will be much easier.

What If It Happens Again?

What if the one we have forgiven hurts us again? What if the very same thing happens again? Will it make what we've done any less real? At first we will no doubt feel hurt, bitter, or angry—or maybe all three. Satan will remind us of our past hurts. We may be tempted to doubt the sincerity of our decision to forgive that person.

If this happens, it is important to remember that forgiveness is an act of the will. The initial decision to forgive the person must be followed by the faith walk of forgiveness. Standing firm on the decision to forgive that person and applying additional forgiveness, if necessary, allow us to replace the hurt and the defeated memories with faith victories. The new offenses can be forgiven as they occur without linking them to past offenses, which have already been forgiven.

Read Luke 17:3-5 in your Bible. How do you think the disciples' plea in verse 5 relates to Jesus' command in verses 3-4?

_____

It is equally important to remember that forgiveness is for our benefit. The other person's behavior may never change. It is up to God, not us, to change that person. It is our responsibility to be set free from the pressure and weight of an unforgiving attitude.

WE WILL KNOW WE HAVE FORGIVEN WHEN . . .

Several things will occur once the forgiveness process is complete. First, our negative feelings will disappear. We will not feel the way we used to feel when we run into these people. Harsh feelings may be replaced by feelings of concern, pity, or empathy, but not resentment.

Second, we will find it much easier to accept the people who have hurt us without feeling the need to change them; we will be willing to take them just the way they are. We will have a new appreciation for their situation once the blinders of resentment have been removed from our eyes. We will understand more why they acted and continue to act the way they do.

Third, our concern about the needs of the other individuals will outweigh our concerns about what they did to us. We will be able to concentrate on them, not on ourselves or our needs.

Forgiveness is a process that can be painful and at times seem unending. Whatever our pain, whatever our situation, we cannot afford to hold on to an unforgiving spirit another day. We must get involved with the process of forgiving others and find out what it means to be really free. If we will persevere and keep our eyes on the One who forgave us, it will be a liberating force like nothing else we have ever experienced.

Read Galatians 5:1 in your Bible. Identify one way you will stand firm against the slavery of unforgiveness.

I will not deny that _____.

I will not be defeated by _____.

I will forgive, accept, and view _____ **as God's tool of growth.**

I will make reconciliation with _____ **by** _____.

To the Leader:

Sometimes Bible study leaders can get their feelings hurt. Perhaps someone left your class or church, perhaps some are not as faithful to attend as they used to be, or perhaps someone made a cutting remark that you've never quite been able to forget. Prayerfully consider whether you have allowed an unforgiving spirit toward one of these persons to develop within you. Then take your hurt to the Lord and apply the five steps of forgiveness from Day 4 to your relationship with the person who has hurt you. Don't just tell yourself you have forgiven him or her— really forgive the person!

Before the Session

1. Provide a loaf of homemade bread (or buy a loaf and pretend it's homemade).
2. Be prepared to summarize 2 Samuel 15.

During the Session

1. Ask: *What aspects of your personality were you just born with and what have you developed over the years? When have you heard people use "I was just born with it" as a cop-out for bad behavior? Is a bitter, unforgiving spirit something people are born with or something they've allowed to develop?*

OR

Invite everyone to enjoy a slice of homemade bread. Ask if participants can describe the process of making bread. [Mix together ingredients, including yeast. Set it aside and let the ingredients work together with the yeast to cause the dough to rise. Punch down the dough, shape it into loaves, let it rise again, and bake.] Remark that if you interrupt the process at any point you don't get bread, and bread is a good thing. But yeast isn't always a good thing in the Bible and is often used to signify sin. Read 1 Corinthians 5:6-8. Comment that in today's lesson Dr. Stanley lists 10 ingredients that, if allowed to blend together and grow, will develop into an unforgiving spirit. He also gives biblical suggestions to stop the process and develop a forgiving spirit instead.

2. Invite someone to state the first two steps toward developing an unforgiving spirit. Discuss the first activity of Day 1. State that this psalm may refer to an incident described in 2 Samuel 15. Briefly summarize the treachery of David's son Absalom from 2 Samuel 15:1-11. Read aloud 2 Samuel 15:12,31 and 16:23–17:3. Ask whether participants think Psalm 55 reflects David's hurt over Absalom's or Ahithophel's [uh-HITH-oh-felz] betrayal. Discuss responses to the last two activities in Day 1. Comment that in 2 Samuel 15:14 we see that David did run away. Ask if participants think that eased his pain. Discuss how people try to detour around the pain of rejection.

Ask why escape leads to an unforgiving spirit rather than to healing. Ask someone to state the last two steps from Day 1. Ask why believers might be prone to get stuck at the denial stage.

3. Ask someone to state from Day 2 the next two steps in developing an unforgiving spirit. Ask how participants see the steps becoming more and more destructive. Ask what participants do when they realize they are traveling on the wrong road. Request they state what persons must do to turn around when they see they are headed toward destruction on the road of unforgiveness. Discuss the last activity in Day 2 to discover how David sought to discover the truth, take responsibility, and be delivered from bitterness against his betrayers.

4. Read the first paragraph of Day 3. Acknowledge: *This seems a little harsh. How is Dr. Stanley actually doing us a favor with these tough words?* Ask the class to identify reasons people are unwilling to forgive. Ask participants which of those excuses they have observed in others or in themselves. Discuss the first activity in Day 3. Ask someone to read Proverbs 16:18 from the margin. Ask: *Who is destroyed by your unwillingness to forgive? Why and how?* Discuss why participants think low self-esteem would make it difficult to forgive and how an unforgiving spirit destroys self-esteem even further. Ask how people can know if they really haven't forgiven someone else. Ask: *Do you think people really don't know how to forgive? Do you think a forgiving spirit is a learned skill or just a good quality some people are lucky enough to be born with?* Declare forgiveness is an act of the will.

5. Ask someone to state the first step in forgiving others. Read Matthew 18:21-34. Ask: *Do you think the slave believed he was fully forgiven? Why or why not? How would the outcome of this story have been different if he believed and accepted the king's complete release of his debt?* Discuss what's involved in the other four steps, allowing volunteers to share how they have followed those steps in forgiving others. Discuss the first activity of Day 5.

6. Request a volunteer read Hebrews 12:1-3. Ask how an unforgiving spirit hinders and entangles believers. Ask: *How can focusing on Christ motivate you to forgive others? How can we know we have truly forgiven them?*

7. Close in prayer, thanking God for His forgiveness and asking that we be able to forgive others who have wronged us.

Forgiving Ourselves

day One

Being Forgiven and *Feeling* Forgiven

Forgiveness is based on the atoning work of the cross and not on anything we do. God's forgiveness does not depend on our confession, nor does His fellowship. Confession is a means for releasing us from the tension and bondage of a guilty conscience. When we pray, *God, You are right. I've sinned against You. I am guilty of this act. I am guilty of that thought,* we achieve release.

Our capacity to enjoy forgiveness—our capacity to enjoy a clean conscience—is based on our willingness to acknowledge and confess our sin. We must come to the point where we are able to forgive ourselves. There will be no peace in our hearts until we forgive ourselves for the wrongs we have committed. *We must be willing to forgive ourselves. Being* forgiven has nothing to do with *feeling* forgiven. *Being* forgiven has to do with what God did for us. *Feeling* forgiven is what this lesson is about.

Lest we think that forgiving ourselves is a modern dilemma, consider Peter and Paul, who had to face the problem of forgiving themselves—in a very intense fashion.

> **Read Luke 22:54-62 in your Bible. If you were Peter, how would you have felt when Jesus turned and looked at you?**

_____

How many times did Peter have to deal with that before he was able to forgive himself? He denied his Lord at a moment in the Lord's life when, if ever the Lord needed a friend, it was then. This was the same Peter who said in effect, "Lord, all the rest of these may forsake You, but when everybody has forsaken You, You can count on the rock." Ironically, Peter was the very one Jesus couldn't count on. Peter had to learn to forgive himself for that.

Then there was Paul before his conversion. His background, learning, and culture, his intensity and commitment to Jehovah God, and his faithfulness to Judaism all had been committed to removing Christianity—that growing, monstrous philosophy—from the face of this earth. He had been consumed with the task of eradicating from people's minds any remains of that person they called Jesus, and Paul had done everything he could to kill or destroy the Lord's church. No doubt the Apostle Paul too grappled with his own forgiveness.

> **Read 1 Corinthians 15:9-10 in your Bible.**
> **How did Paul demonstrate that he regretted his earlier actions?**

_____

> **How did he demonstrate that he had forgiven himself?**

_____

Many of us are at—or have been at—that place in our lives. We struggle with forgiving ourselves for things we did in the past—some of those mistakes having occurred years and years ago. *Yet the ability or capacity to forgive ourselves is absolutely essential if any peace whatsoever is to be found.*

day Two

Negative Consequences of Not Forgiving Ourselves, Part 1

The problem is that some of us are not able to forgive ourselves. We look at whatever we've done and think that we are beyond forgiveness. But what we really feel is disappointment in ourselves—a disappointment that confuses measurement of our sin with merit for our forgiveness.

Sin and self-forgiveness tend to assume inverse proportions in our minds—that is, the greater our sin, the lesser our forgiveness. Similarly, the lesser our sin, the greater our forgiveness. Although some sins bring greater condemnation or chastisement in the life of believers, God's viewpoint is that sin is sin. And just as God's viewpoint of sin covers all sins, so does His viewpoint of forgiveness. But when we choose not to forgive ourselves as God does, we can expect to experience the following consequences of a self-directed unforgiving spirit.

SELF-PUNISHMENT

The first consequence of a self-directed unforgiving spirit is that *we punish ourselves on an ongoing basis*. How do we do that? We replay our sins continually. We even replay the feelings of guilt. And as we do, we put ourselves in a tortured state that God never intended.

If, for instance, we wake up in the morning under a load of guilt, we have put the burden on ourselves, not on God. We are unwilling to forgive ourselves, even though as believers and children of God we are already forgiven. We get up, work, play, go to bed, and sleep in a self-imposed bondage, in a prison we build ourselves.

We spiritually incarcerate ourselves despite the fact that *no* place in the Bible does God say He has forgiven us of all our sins "except . . ." Jesus paid it all. Jesus bore in His body the price for *all* our sins. No exceptions.

> **Read Psalm 25:6-7 in your Bible.**
> **What do you remember most often?**
> ❑ **Your past sins**
> ❑ **God's grace and mercy**
>
> **What does God remember?**
> ❑ **Your past sins**
> ❑ **His love for you**

UNCERTAINTY

The second consequence of a self-directed unforgiving spirit is that *we live under a cloud of uncertainty*. We do not accept our forgiveness by God; we exist under an abiding question mark. If we never forgive ourselves, we can never be confident God has forgiven us—and we bear the weight of this guilt. We are not quite sure where we stand with God. We are not quite sure what He may do next because we are not worthy of His blessing. And so we pass up the peace that passes all understanding and we have no contentment.

If we refuse to forgive ourselves—despite the fact that God has *not* dealt with us according to our sins, that God has *not* rewarded us according to our iniquities—we continue to live under that cloud of uncertainty.

SENSE OF UNWORTHINESS

The third consequence of a self-directed unforgiving spirit is that *we develop a sense of unworthiness.* Because we are guilty, we also feel unworthy.

But when we hold ourselves accountable for our sins, we are indulging in a guilt trip. Satan encourages guilt trips. He may inject these ideas in our thoughts: *Why should God answer my prayer? He is not going to hear what I am saying. Look what I have done.* Satan punches the button, and we replay the past sin. Satan keeps getting us to replay in our minds what God says He has forgotten—and we guiltily oblige. And each time we replay the past sin by not forgiving ourselves, our faith takes a beating and we feel unworthy. This sense of unworthiness affects our prayer life, our intimate relationship with God, and our service for Him.

> **Read 1 John 3:21-22a in your Bible. In the margin, rewrite these verses negatively to describe persons who won't forgive themselves.**

To a great degree we paralyze our usefulness before God when we allow our guilt to cause us to feebly—and always unsuccessfully—attempt payment for our sins when Jesus already paid the debt two thousand years ago for *all* our sins.

> **Read 1 John 3:20 in the margin. Underline which entity is greater. Circle which one you are going to live by.**
>
> **Your guilty conscience   OR   God's forgiveness**

"Our heart may say that we have done wrong. But remember, God is greater than our heart" (1 John 3:20, NKJV).

Negative Consequences of Not Forgiving Ourselves, Part 2

EXCESSIVE BEHAVIOR

The fourth consequence of a self-directed unforgiving spirit is that *we attempt to overcome our guilt by compulsive behavior and excesses in our lives.*

Some of us even try to escape from the incessant self-pronouncements of guilt by investing huge amounts of energy into our work for the Lord—we work harder, faster, longer. But no matter how furiously we work, our guilt cannot be diminished by our frantic pace. Sometimes we take on two, three, or four jobs in the church to prove our dedication. We teach Sunday school, sing in the choir, and visit the homebound. What servants of God! And we end up making nervous wrecks of ourselves.

> "For I am ready to fall, And my sorrow is continually before me. For I confess my iniquity; I am full of anxiety because of my sin" (Ps. 38:17-18).

As you read Psalm 38:17-18 in the margin underline what you have in common with the psalmist.

Compulsive behavior of this sort is akin to saying, "God, I want to thank You for Jesus' death on the cross, but it wasn't enough." So because we do not accept God's forgiveness, we double our efforts. (Do we really think that God wasn't able to do it alone? That He needs *our* help?) And we begin a self-feeding, spiritually defeating cycle.

The only real answer to our dilemma is to accept God's forgiveness and to forgive ourselves. We may think, *I can't forgive myself for what I have done.* But God gave us the rebuttal to that type of thinking. When Jesus took our sins upon Himself, it's as if He said, "I have come to liberate you. I have come to free you. I have come to set the captives free." If we do not forgive ourselves because of our unworthiness, we miss the point of Jesus' death on the cross.

FALSE HUMILITY

The fifth consequence of a self-directed unforgiving spirit is that *we develop a false sense of humility when we feel permanently judged guilty and sentenced by God.* We wear but a facade of humility when we declare ourselves so unworthy to serve God. And our "humble face" serves as a mask to keep us from seeing our true face.

Does this sound familiar? We may be complimented: "That was absolutely marvelous!" But then we respond, "I don't deserve your praise. Just give God all the praise and the glory." Sometimes that's a sincere response, but sometimes that's a response motivated by a guilty complex. When we harbor a false sense of humility, it's very difficult to accept a compliment.

It is amazing how a self-directed unforgiving spirit distorts our viewpoint and perverts our thinking. It makes us harbor and nourish—even covet—our past errors so that we wallow in fake humility. We become focused on ourselves and on our unworthiness and on our humility.

SELF-DEPRIVATION

The sixth consequence of a self-directed unforgiving spirit is that *we deprive ourselves of things God wants us to enjoy.* Self-deprivation is the opposite of compulsive behavior and excesses. We say things like, "Oh, I couldn't buy myself that. I couldn't go there. I couldn't do that."

Self-deprivation is like an acid that eats away at the truth of Jesus' sacrifice. We do not achieve a state of forgiveness by arbitrarily abstaining from good things in our lives. God does not ask us to deprive ourselves in order to "deserve" forgiveness. Self-deprivation is self-choice, not God's choice. Do we presume to know something about our sin that God does not know? Do we dare think that we have some new information about sin and forgiveness that God does not have? Of course not. If our sovereign, holy, righteous God has seen fit in His omniscience to declare us not guilty and to forgive us our sin, we have no grounds for self-deprivation.

To deny ourselves forgiveness and to put ourselves through unending punishment is to sentence ourselves to hell on earth. Satan is a master at deception, and it is Satan who makes us think that we have to suffer until God says, "OK, that's enough." At what point do we think we will be free? When will we have suffered enough? It is apparent that this type of thinking is absurd, yet many believers act as if they think that's how God's forgiveness works.

Read John 10:10 in your Bible. Which statement best describes your life?
❏ **Because I won't forgive myself, Satan is stealing my joy, killing my hope, and destroying my life.**
❏ **Because I have accepted God's forgiveness, I am experiencing the full life Christ came to give me.**

day *Four*

Why We Can't Forgive Ourselves

Since we know the negative consequences from not forgiving ourselves, what stands in our way? What hinders our acceptance of God's forgiveness on our own behalf? Our resistance generally can be traced to one of four general problem areas: (1) belief in performance-based forgiveness; (2) disappointment in self; (3) adjustment and surrender to guilt; and (4) expectation of repeated sin.

BELIEF IN PERFORMANCE-BASED FORGIVENESS

Performance-based forgiveness is not biblically based forgiveness. We can't "pay" for God's unlimited forgiveness by working harder or by serving more fervently. The Bible says that God accepts us on the basis of what He did, not on the basis of what we try to do. But we tend to rationalize. *I have got to measure up*. Ever since we were children, we have learned that whatever we achieve or receive we do so as a result of our own actions.

"Mom, can I have a cookie?"

"If you are good."

Performance. Our whole lives are based on performance. *If I clean my room, Mom will let me do this. If I take out the trash, Dad will let me do that. If I do well at the tryouts, I may make the team.*

Then, when it comes to the grace of God and the Bible's teachings, what happens? No performance is required. *Hold it*, we may think. *That isn't right.* But it is right—God's idea of forgiveness is in a category all by itself.

As believers, we are forgiven children of God, no matter what we do. This does *not* mean that we can do whatever we like and go merrily on our way. It means that as believers we have already been forgiven of our sins—past, present, and future—whether we confess them or not. We don't have to keep asking for forgiveness and keep working to pay for it.

Our difficulty is not one of being unforgiven; it is one of *feeling* unforgiven. We are separated from God by sin, not by lack of forgiveness. Believers are always forgiven. Grace is an unmerited, undeserved, nonnegotiable gift from God that comes to us prepaid. It can't be purchased, and it is offered freely to all who receive it. That's what the grace of God is all about.

> **Read Ephesians 2:8-9 in your Bible. Fill in the blanks to make a true statement. My forgiveness has everything to do with _____ and nothing to do with**
>
> **_____.**
>
> **Now say this out loud until you believe it!**

DISAPPOINTMENT IN SELF

We sometimes have a difficult time accepting the truth about ourselves. I can remember a personal experience where God had done a marvelous work in my life. The Lord was blessing me, and I was just moving right along. Then I acted in a very disappointing way. I knew better, but I blew it horribly. The Lord had lifted me up, and I fell flat on my face. I still remember the feelings of shame and depression.

I wrestled with God's forgiveness for a short period of time before I was able to accept it. At least I thought I accepted it. Because I had sorely disappointed myself, it was difficult for me to forgive myself for not living up to my own expectations.

It is important to realize that we disappoint ourselves; we don't disappoint God. How can we disappoint someone who already knows what we're going to do? Disappointment is the result of unfulfilled expectations, and God doesn't expect anything of us. God knows that we are going to blow it. That's what the grace of God is all about.

ADJUSTMENT AND SURRENDER TO GUILT

Emotionally, we may live so long under guilt and self-condemnation that the very idea of being free is threatening. We feel comfortable with what we know, and what we know is guilt. We adjust to our feelings of guilt and surrender the peace we could enjoy if we forgave ourselves.

I have counseled people and clearly outlined what the Bible has to say about their particular problem. After professing understanding, these same people may end up praying the same old prayer they pray all the time, and when they finish praying, they haven't dealt with the issue.

If we want to be released from guilt, we must change our thinking. We need a thorough cleansing of our thought processes. No more thinking, *I know what the Bible says about forgiveness, but—*. Every time we include a *but*, we put one more bar in our prison of guilt. We need to get rid of the bars; we need to break out of the prison. We don't have to be there. But we have to want to get out.

EXPECTATION OF REPEATED SIN

I know God could forgive me. And I know He has forgiven me. I guess the reason I don't forgive myself is that I know I am going to repeat that sin. These are the thoughts that cause us so much trouble.

How many sins did we commit before the cross? We weren't even in existence two thousand years ago. All *our* sins for which Christ died were in the future, including sins that we commit over and over again. God's forgiveness is all-inclusive, regardless of the nature of our sins or the frequency of our indulgence.

This does *not* mean we escape the consequences of our sins simply because we are forgiven. This means that we are assured forever of forgiveness, that we need not withhold forgiveness from ourselves because we may sin again. God forgives us every time for every sin, and so must we.

Read Romans 7:21-25.

Can you identify with Paul's feelings of wretchedness?
❑ **Yes** ❑ **No** ❑ **Sometimes**

What did Paul acknowledge was the only remedy for his past, present, and future sins?

_____

Have you accepted that remedy for ALL your sins as well? ❑ **Yes** ❑ **No**

How We Can Forgive Ourselves

Micah 7:18-19

God delights to show me mercy and has hurled my sin into the deepest part of the sea where it can never be retrieved.

How do we forgive ourselves? Regardless of how long we have been in bondage, we can be free if we follow four biblical steps.

STEP 1. RECOGNIZE THE PROBLEM

We must recognize and acknowledge that we have not forgiven ourselves. We must come to grips with the fact that we still hold ourselves in bondage.

Psalm 103:1-5

_____

_____

_____

STEP 2. REPENT OF SIN

We must repent of that sin for which we cannot forgive ourselves. We must tell God that we realize that our unwillingness to forgive ourselves is not in keeping with His Word. And we must thank Him for His forgiveness as we confess our sin to Him.

Psalm 130:3-4

_____

_____

_____

STEP 3. REAFFIRM TRUST

We must reaffirm our trust in the testimony of Scripture: "As far as the east is from the west, so far has He removed our transgressions from us" (Ps. 103:12, NKJV).

John 8:10-11

_____

_____

_____

STEP 4. CONFESS FREEDOM AND CHOOSE TO RECEIVE IT

We must confess our freedom and in faith choose to receive it freely on the basis of God's Word and as an act of our will.

Romans 8:1-2

_____

_____

_____

If we are willing to follow these simple steps, not only will we be set free, but the healing process will be initiated. When we choose by an act of the will to accept what God has said is true, we accept God's acceptance of us. We have played back that accusing videotape for the last time. We are free.

Romans 8:32-35

_____

_____

_____

Read the Scripture passages listed in the margin. Write a personal statement about God and your sins using the truths from each Scripture. An example is given.

leader Guide

To the Leader:

Are there class members who have been absent for quite some time? Ask God to reveal to you how you can let those members know they will be welcomed back to class with open arms. Be sure to act on what God tells you.

During the Session

1. Relate this story: *Once a farmer found a baby eagle and took it home to live with his chickens. The eagle grew up acting like a chicken. One day the farmer decided it was time for the bird to act like an eagle. But no matter how many times he threw that eagle off the top of the barn, it simply dropped to the earth and began scratching like a chicken.* Ask: *What determined how the eagle behaved—what he really was or what he felt he was?* State that as long as the eagle felt he was a chicken, he would never soar like an eagle. Ask: *What determines how believers behave—the truth that they are completely forgiven or their feelings of not being forgiven? Why?* State the purpose of this week's lesson is to help believers forgive themselves so they won't just be forgiven but will also feel forgiven and soar as God intended.

   OR

   Ask why people enjoy watching TV shows that feature home videos. Ask if participants have any home videos of their own humorous mistakes and misfortunes and invite them to describe them. (If possible, show a short one of your own funny family videos.) Inquire: *It's understandable why we would replay these fun videos repeatedly, but why do we keep replaying our mistakes and sins over and over in our minds?* Comment that in this week's study Dr. Stanley urges us to forgive ourselves and to destroy those destructive videotapes.

2. Discuss the first activity of Day 1. Ask what Peter probably played over and over in his mind after the incident described. Invite someone to read John 21:15-19. Explain that this passage often is interpreted as Jesus' indication of complete forgiveness of Peter. Ask: *Who else do you think forgave Peter that day?* Request someone read Acts 2:37-41. Discuss whether participants think Peter could have preached so powerfully if he hadn't forgiven himself for denying Christ.

3. Remark that ineffectiveness in God's kingdom results from the many negative consequences of not forgiving oneself. Request participants state the first negative consequence discussed in Day 2. Discuss the first activity of Day 2. Discuss: *How can we replace our condemning memories of past sins with memories of God's grace and mercy?*

4. Invite volunteers to describe days when they have felt like they were under a cloud. Remark that we can't always help clouds of misfortune that tend to rain on us at times, but an unforgiving spirit toward ourselves leads to a cloud of uncertainty. Help participants explore what Dr. Stanley meant by that cloud of uncertainty. Discuss the third consequence of not forgiving ourselves. Read 1 John 3:18-23 and discuss the second activity of Day 2. Ask how we can gain the confidence to stand before God when our hearts are so burdened with guilt. Request someone read 1 Corinthians 4:3-4. Ask: *Whose judgment was the only one that mattered to Paul?* Declare: *It doesn't matter if others say you are guilty; it doesn't matter if you think you are guilty. If you have given your life to Christ, God declares you are not guilty and He is the only true Judge.*

5. Ask if participants ever had an aunt or grandmother who felt they never ate enough and continued to pile food on their plates. Ask how that illustrates (albeit imperfectly) a person who attempts to overcome guilt by excessive behavior. Ask: *If we have too much on our plates and keep piling on more activities, what do we need to do?* Ask participants to describe (without mentioning names) how they have observed believers displaying any of the negative consequences of a self-directed unforgiving spirit discussed in Days 2 and 3.

6. Discuss why a guilty conscience makes us ineffective in God's kingdom. Comment that we can only work for God's kingdom when we're free; we cannot be effective when we live in a prison of guilt and self-condemnation. Ask what four hindrances Dr. Stanley declared are the bars that keep us in that prison. Discuss the learning activities in Day 4.

7. Lead a discussion on how we as believers can practically apply the steps toward forgiving ourselves in Day 5. As time allows, read the Scripture passages listed in the margin at the end of Day 5. Discuss how the truths in each passage can empower believers to forgive themselves.

8. Close in prayer.

Bitterness and How to Deal with It

day One

The Root of Bitterness

Bitterness often lies beneath our inability to forgive and be forgiven. It is a corrosive culprit that denies our peace and destroys our relationships.

> "See to it that no one comes short of the grace of God; that no root of bitterness springing up causes trouble, and by it many be defiled" (Heb. 12:15).

Read Hebrews 12:15 from the margin. What metaphor did the writer use to describe bitterness?
❏ **Poison root**   ❏ **Sword**   ❏ **Fruit**   ❏ **Acid**

The Greek word for *bitterness (pikria)* comes from the root word *pik,* which means "to cut," and therefore, "pointed" or "sharp." It refers to what is cutting and sharp. It also implies "bitter taste." Verse 15 refers metaphorically to bitter fruit produced by the root of bitterness.

As I have counseled hurting people, I have helped them discover bitter roots they had been nurturing for weeks, months, and often years. We can be bitter and hide it from the rest of the world by disguising it as various other attitudes. We express bitterness in our lives in a number of ways—anger, passion, slander, malice. But we cannot hide our bitterness from God or even from our own bodies.

Bitterness is *never* constructive; bitterness is *always* destructive. It doesn't make any difference what people have done to us or how bad it was or how often they did it. Bitterness as a response to wrongdoing is never acceptable before God. Nothing good ever comes from bitterness.

"*See to it.*" That is, be diligent. The word *see,* as it is used in verse 15, is derived from the same combination of Greek roots—*epi* ("upon") and *skopeo* ("to look at," "contemplate")—that gives us the word *oversight.* As Christians, we are charged with a duty to fulfill.

"*That no one comes short of the grace of God.*" We are to care for one another and see to it that we live in grace. We are to respond *in* grace *to* grace. We can't allow ourselves to slip over into our old lifestyles. As Christians, we can no longer respond to hurts, abuse, cheating, criticism, lies, and rejection in any way other than how our Lord responds to us—with forgiveness.

"*That no root of bitterness springing up.*" The day we received Jesus as our Savior, we forsook all rights to be bitter. We must put all bitterness from us and guard against its taking root in our lives—no matter what happens, no matter how despicably we are treated.

Read Ephesians 4:30-32 in your Bible. Complete the chart below.

We grieve God when	We please God when

We tend to think that individual, personal circumstances are clearly exceptions. A deliberate smear campaign against us, for instance. Or a husband who walks out on his 43 year old wife and takes up with a 21 year old. Or a wife who betrays her husband for the fleeting sensation of a weekend affair. Or children who reject their parents' values and play the life of idle degenerates after having been brought up in godly homes. Or women who are held back in the corporate world because they're the wrong gender. Or men who are passed over for promotion because they're the wrong color. Or employees who are fired to make room for the boss's friends and family members. Or retirees who are struck with severe disability after having waited years to enjoy the fruits of their labor.

Bitterness can be "justified" so easily. *Well, I have a right to be bitter. He knew I was after that account, and just when I was about to close the deal, he lied about my qualifications. That cost me a bundle, and I'm sure not going to smile and say it's OK. He hurt me, and he's not going to get away with it.* We must be careful not to allow bitterness to take root in our lives. As a root has fine tentacles that reach out for moisture in order to grow, so does a root of bitterness have tentacles that reach out. The root of bitterness needs feedback, little evidences of its right for existence, in order to grow. It is fed by our misconceived notions that we have a "right" to feel bitter. But the truth is that believers have no right to respond with bitterness.

**Have you been watering a bitter root with excuses
and justifications?** ❑ **Yes** ❑ **No** ❑ **I'm not sure**
**If yes, briefly describe why you have decided you
have the right to be bitter.**

_____

**What good has your assumed right to feel bitter done
for you?**

_____

If we allow bitterness to take root, we relinquish control of our lives.
We cannot live with bitterness because bitterness will eat away at us until
we are destroyed.

day Two

The Effects of Bitterness

**Reread Hebrews 12:15 from the margin of Day 1.
What does bitterness do?**

_____

We may not even be consciously aware that we are nursing bitter feelings,
but the effects of bitterness are subtle and many.

PHYSICAL ILLNESSES

Bitterness is like a continually running machine that uses our bodies
for its energy source. It runs when we are sleeping, it runs when we are
talking with our friends, and it runs when we are simply sitting and being
quiet. Because bitterness is a lifestyle and not an isolated occurrence,
it never shuts down. It keeps operating and draining energy.

It is impossible to be bitter very long without it affecting our bodies.
More and more, medical professionals are beginning to see some kind of
link between the way our bodies function and the way we think.
Bitterness, anger, and other negative emotions have been associated with
glandular problems, high blood pressure, cardiac disorders, ulcers, and a
host of other physical ailments.

WE STAINED RELATIONSHIPS

Bitterness causes one person trouble and defiles others. As used in Hebrews 12:15, the Greek word for defile *(miaino)* means "to stain" or "to dye." The bitterness we nourish will stain our relationships. This is one reason why there are so many separations, divorces, and broken homes.

Much of the time the cause of such problems is found to be an unforgiving spirit that has taken bitter root. Bitterness can paralyze us. Even when we genuinely want to love another person, we can't. Deep inside we may find ourselves infected by roots of bitterness and resentment, even simmering hatred.

Bitterness has so many little sprouts to it. Distrust is one of them. Insecurity is another. When the Bible says "see to it that . . . no root of bitterness (springs) up," it is because the consequences are awesome and ongoing.

> **Read Acts 8:20-23 in your Bible. How might others see that you are full of bitterness (or how have you observed that bitter root in others)?**
> ❑ **Physical illness**   ❑ **Anger**   ❑ **Distrust**
> ❑ **Insecurity**   ❑ **Resentment**   ❑ **Greed**
> ❑ **Stained relationships**   ❑ **Other:** _____

SPIRITUAL STUMBLING BLOCKS

Bitterness creates a cloak of guilt. We know we shouldn't feel the way we do toward others, and we know God doesn't want us to be full of resentment. And, our reasoning goes, if God isn't pleased with us, how can He accept us? We sense a barrier between God and ourselves and begin to doubt our salvation. How in the world are we going to be secure in our salvation when this turmoil, this civil war, is constantly going on?

Bitterness also hinders our influence for Christ. What kind of Christian testimony can we have if we are bitter toward God and toward our neighbors? How can we convincingly talk to others about the forgiveness of God when we refuse to forgive those who have wronged us? When we allow bitterness to take over our lives, that bitterness spills over into the lives of those around us.

How many of us harbor those little things that caused us to feel rejected? How many of us today are angry adults because we don't feel loved?

As we think of those who have hurt us or wronged us, we need to deal with those feelings. Some things may have been said or done long ago, so long ago that we don't think we feel their sting anymore, but our thoughts are affected. An unforgiving spirit is a devastating emotion that none of us can afford.

Bitterness eventually develops into scheming and plotting. We begin to manipulate events that are harmful to the other party. We arrive at the point where we would like to inflict all the vengeance possible on that person. If we can't, then maybe somebody else can. We just stand back and smile. I have heard of men and women who divorced their spouses years ago and yet are still scheming to get their vengeance. They are still hoping that circumstances will destroy the former spouses in some form or fashion.

When bitterness becomes our master, we act foolishly and irrationally. Bitter, angry parents often fling verbal javelins at their children, shattering their children's self-esteem, their sense of belonging, their sense of competency. Parents, impelled by bitter attitudes, can destroy their children with bitter attitudes.

We have looked at some of the negative effects of a bitter spirit. Read Romans 12:14-21 in your Bible and list some of the positive effects of a forgiving spirit.

Recovery from Bitterness

How can we recover from the effects of bitterness? *Recover* means "to get back" or "to regain." To recover from an illness, for example, means to get back or regain one's health. To recover from bitterness, then, means to get back or regain one's sweet or even temper.

When the root of bitterness has been growing a long time, its removal is not always instantaneous. A husband and wife who decide to get back together after having been separated can honestly confess to each other and repent of their sins, but full restoration comes gradually. The inner healing of the spirit sometimes takes longer than the physical healing of a broken arm or leg. We may have lived with damaged emotions for years, perhaps since childhood. As children of God, however, we have the capacity to forgive and to root out bitterness from our lives, even when it causes us temporary loss or humiliation. Unless we forgive, we cannot love.

> "As children of God we have the capacity to forgive and to root out bitterness from our lives."—Charles Stanley

Does the bitterness inside you seem more like:
❑ **An army of enemy soldiers intent on destroying you?**
❑ **A huge barrier you can't get over?**

Read Psalm 18:29 in your Bible. Can you conquer that army or get over that barrier? ❑ **Yes** ❑ **No**

How? _____

GETTING MOTIVATED TO DEAL WITH BITTERNESS

How can we be motivated to forgive and to root out bitterness? We need to heed the call of our Lord Jesus Christ to forgive others.

Read Luke 6:36-37 in your Bible and complete each statement:
Be merciful like _____.
Don't judge so_____.
Don't condemn so _____.
Forgive so_____.

Jesus did not mean that our Heavenly Father will not forgive us if we haven't forgiven others. Jesus meant that if we don't emotionally release those who have wronged us, God will keep the pressure on us until we do, because He wants us to be reconciled.

When we fully comprehend God's forgiveness toward us, we simply cannot justify our holding anyone else accountable. Throughout Jesus' ministry, He consistently taught forgiveness. But not only did He proclaim it, He demonstrated it with His words from the cross: "Father, forgive them; for they do not know what they are doing" (Luke 23:34).

Because Christ dwells in us as believers, we have a spiritual nature to forgive. We received this new spiritual nature when we received Christ. The life we live is an expression of the life of Christ. We have the capacity to forgive when we have been deeply hurt because Christ within us is able to release through us forgiveness toward anyone. Just as Jesus forgave those who crucified Him, His life within us makes it possible for us to forgive all kinds of hurt and abuse, even in the most heinous forms. Because we are children of God, it is out of character for us to have unforgiving spirits and allow bitter roots to take hold. Jesus never withheld forgiveness, so too we should never withhold forgiveness. By faith we can allow Christ to express that forgiveness through us toward others.

As we forgive one another, we release ourselves from bitterness. Emotional release enables physical and spiritual healing, and it frees us from bondage to other people. As we forgive one another, we enjoy reconciliation and the joy of healthy, loving relationships.

> "You are God's chosen people. You are holy and dearly loved.
> So put on tender mercy and kindness as if they were your clothes.
> Don't be proud.
> Be gentle and patient.
> Put up with each other.
> Forgive the things you are holding against one another. Forgive, just as the Lord forgave you"
> (Col. 3:12-13, NIRV).

Read Colossians 3:12-13 from the margin. Freedom, healing, and loving relationships result when believers put on _____ and put up with _____.

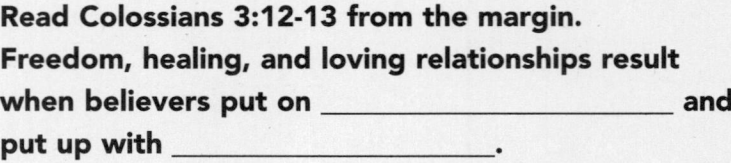

day Four

Getting Rid of Bitterness

Getting rid of bitterness is a step-by-step process that leads toward emotional liberation and spiritual freedom. The steps are simple. As you are reading this, the face of someone toward whom you feel bitter has probably come to mind. Keep that person(s) in mind as you continue.

1. Make a list of the ways in which that person has offended you.
2. Make a list of your own faults.
3. Make a list of things you have done and for which God has forgiven you.
4. Ask God to help you view that person who has wronged you as a tool in the hand of God.
5. Ask God to forgive you for your bitterness toward that person.
6. Decide in your heart to assume total responsibility for your attitude.

7. If you feel it is appropriate and will not cause more problems than it solves, go to that person, confess your bitterness, and ask for forgiveness. Remember, you are assuming the responsibility for your attitude; you are not trying to solicit repentance.

8. We have but two choices: We can allow bitterness to destroy us, or we can allow God to develop us into the persons He wants us to be. We must choose to view our circumstances and hurts as tools to be used by God to further develop our spiritual lives.

Now that you have dug out the root of bitterness, note from the Scriptures below ways you can develop a healthy root system.

Jeremiah 17:7-8 _____

Ephesians 3:14-19 _____

Colossians 2:6-7 _____

day *Five*

To Forgive Or Not To Forgive, That Is the Question

Forgiveness is liberating, but it is also sometimes painful. It is liberating because we are freed from the heavy load of guilt, bitterness, and anger we have harbored within. It is painful because it is difficult to have to face ourselves, God, and others with our failures. It seems easier to blame others and go on defending our position of being right, even though we continue to hurt. But the poison of an unforgiving spirit that permeates our entire lives, separating us from God and friends, can never be adequately defended. It is devastating to our spiritual and emotional well-being and to our physical health.

Read a biblical demonstration of forgiveness in Numbers 12:1-13 and answer the items on page 166:

How did Aaron and Miriam sin against Moses?

_____

List emotions Moses may have experienced after such treatment by his brother and sister.

_____

If Moses had not had a forgiving spirit, how might he have responded to Miriam's punishment?

_____

Who would have benefited from that unforgiving response?

_____

What principles of forgiveness that you have learned in this seven-week study do you observe in Moses?

_____

If you have enjoyed these studies from Charles Stanley and desire to purchase your own copy of his book *The Gift of Forgiveness* to read and study in greater detail, visit the LifeWay Christian Store serving you. Or you can order a copy by calling 1-800-233-1123.

Has there ever been a time in your life when you came to grips with your rebellion against God, acknowledged your need of His forgiveness, and trusted Christ as your personal Savior? Are you keeping short accounts with Him? That is, when you disobey Him, do you confess it immediately and walk on in His Spirit, enjoying your fellowship with Him?

Are you still unable to forgive someone who hurt you deeply and you still bear the scars? How long will you remain a prisoner to your own unforgiving spirit? You have within you the power to forgive, to be healed, and to be set free to live your life to the fullest.

Before you finish these lessons from *The Gift of Forgiveness*, forgive the one who has hurt you even as your Heavenly Father has forgiven you, and *be really free!*

Will you choose to allow hurtful circumstances or people make you: Bitter?   OR   Better? (Circle one.)

What actions will you take to reflect your choice?

_____

_____

Before the Session

Dig up a dandelion and its roots and bring it to class.

During the Session

1. Read Hebrews 12:15 and Dr. Stanley's statement from the end of Day 1: "If we allow bitterness to take root, we relinquish control of our lives." Ask learners why they agree or disagree with that statement.

OR

Ask participants which of the following they think would be most destructive to a person and why: being stabbed with a sword, ingesting drain cleaner, drinking arsenic, or holding onto bitterness.

FOR EITHER OPTION: Discuss how any of the metaphors listed in the first activity of Day 1 could describe bitterness. Ask why participants think the writer of Hebrews chose to describe bitterness as *a root.*

2. If possible, display a dandelion and its roots. Ask if participants have more grass or dandelions in their yards. Discuss how one can prevent weeds from taking over a lawn. Acknowledge weed-free landscaping requires diligent effort. Request learners read the phrase from Hebrews 12:15 that admonishes believers to apply diligence to keep bitterness from taking root. Remark that some people tend to put more effort into nurturing bitterness. Discuss how people nurture bitterness. Ask what Hebrews 12:15 declares is the result of nurturing bitterness. Ask: *How do we miss the grace of God if we allow bitterness to take root in our lives?* Ask participants to identify ways people tend to excuse or justify bitter feelings. Ask: *Do you think some of those justifications are legitimate? What do we do to God when we nurse bitterness?* [See Eph. 4:30-32.] *Why does God grieve when we are bitter?*

3. Comment that one reason God grieves is because He knows what bitterness does to His beloved children. Discuss the first activity of Day 2. Note that Dr. Stanley compared bitterness to a constantly running machine. Discuss how bitterness affects how a person sleeps, works, talks, and even relaxes. Explore what Dr. Stanley meant by "stained relationships." Ask someone to read Acts 8:9-24. Discuss what

To the Leader:

This study may have stirred up emotions participants thought they had buried or dealt with long ago. Pray about how you can support participants who are striving to apply what they have learned about forgiveness so they can truly be free to enjoy life and serve as God intended.

Contact all participants, prospects, and absentees and encourage them to be present next week as you begin your study of *The Love Languages of God* by Gary Chapman.

may have led to Simon's bitterness. Ask how participants think Peter could see that bitterness. Invite participants to state how they have seen bitterness in others (without naming names).

4. State that bitterness negatively affects a person physically and relationally. Ask how bitterness hurts a believer spiritually. Ask Dr. Stanley's questions: *What kind of Christian witness do we have if we are bitter toward God and toward others? How can we convincingly talk to others about God's forgiveness when we refuse to forgive others?* Discuss how bitterness continues to develop and destroy. Discuss the last activity of Day 2. Remark that a forgiving spirit leads to the kind of believer described in Romans 12:9-13. Read those verses. Declare that description should motivate every believer to get rid of bitterness and learn to forgive as Christ forgives.

5. Comment that Jesus' words in Luke 6:36-37 give us further motivation to deal with bitterness. Discuss the second activity in Day 3. Explore what Jesus meant when He declared, "Forgive, and you will be forgiven." Ask learners to state things that are easier said than done. [Samples: put together a swing set, prepare a meal.] Ask if "be merciful, don't judge or condemn, and forgive" is easier said than done, and why. Request someone read the quotation in the margin of Day 3. Ask why we have the capacity to undertake this difficult task of forgiveness. Ask: *When has someone encouraged you with the simple phrase, "You can do it"?* Encourage volunteers to share verses that have assured them they can do difficult tasks, including forgiving others. Be prepared to share some verses that motivate and encourage you.

6. Display the dandelion and ask how to get a dandelion out of the ground. Acknowledge uprooting a dandelion can't be accomplished with a halfhearted pull; it requires effort to dig it out. State that the steps to get rid of bitterness require a wholehearted effort. Go over those steps in Day 4, inviting volunteers to add comments or suggestions. Work together to complete the activity in Day 4. Discuss how confident trust in and gratitude for God's power and love can help believers weed out hurts before they develop into bitter roots.

7. As time permits, discuss the first activity in Day 5.

8. Invite participants to share which principles of forgiveness they have learned in this study have been the most challenging or meaningful to them. Close in prayer.